Disasters
Earth Upheavals
Dying

God Gave Warning In Time

Disasters
Earth Upheavals
Dying

God Gave Warning In Time

THE WORD
THE UNIVERSAL SPIRIT

First Edition, 2009
Published by:
© Universal Life
The Inner Religion
PO Box 3549
Woodbridge, CT 06525
U S A

Translated from the original German title:
Katastrophen, Erdumwälzungen, Sterben
Gott hat rechtzeitig gewarnt
(3rd Expanded Edition May 2008)

Order No. S 445en

From the Universal Life Series
with the consent of
© Verlag DAS WORT GmbH
Max-Braun-Str. 2
97828 Marktheidenfeld, Germany

ISBN 978-1-890841-63-8

Table of Contents

Introduction

The topic of disasters, above all in connection with the climate change, ranks much higher in public awareness and the media than it did a few years ago. We no longer read only about dramatic individual natural disasters and their consequences; scientists are now pointing out ever more clearly that the climate change, whose dramatic effects are increasingly coming to light, is caused by human beings. The explosive nature of the numerous research results during recent years has stimulated us to publish this book. Everyone can follow the rapidly progressing development; hardly a day goes by without new reports and events reaching the public eye. These reports and events help expand our awareness of the increasingly dramatic and obvious colossal extent of the threatening intensification of the condition of our earth.

Considering the fact that it is becoming more and more evident in what direction the ship-world is drifting, the question arises: Has humankind fallen victim to a kind of "Titanic syndrome"? Mega-concerts are put on to create an "awareness of the climate change," and meetings of politicians convey the impression that a sustainable solution to the problem can be found. Reality looks very different. Really, should only a few be aware of the gravity of the situation on our planet?

Presented here are just a few headlines from the media, which make it clear where the world stands. They are not the individual reports of storms, floods, droughts, earthquakes … which appear day after day and thus, would soon be forgotten after this book is printed. More and more often and ever more clearly, apparently irreversible global phenomena, trends, developments and escalations are pointed out, whose effects and consequences far exceed our ability to comprehend. Examples are as follows:

- Super-volcano: A bang that devastates continents. Researchers believe that the possibility of an eruption of a super-volcano is totally realistic during this century. In Europe alone two gigantic volcanoes are waiting for their next eruption. (Süddeutschezeitung, Mar. 9, 2005)

- Livestock heats up the greenhouse. Livestock production is one of the main causes of the greenhouse effect – what can be done? (taz.de, Feb. 23, 2007)

- Four out of ten people die of environmental pollution. According to calculations made by US researchers, more than a third of all deaths are caused by contamination of the environment with chemicals and poisons. Ecological damage can cause undernourishment, malaria, diarrhea and respiratory illnesses – which can be fatal. (Spiegel Online, Aug. 14, 2007)

- Threat to a diversity of species: Global warming could trigger mass dying. (Spiegel Online, Oct. 24, 2007)

- The world is becoming dangerous to life. In a report by the environmental program of the United Nations (UNEP), scientists warn that the dramatic state of the environment threatens the survival of humankind. (Süddeutschezeitung, Oct. 25, 2007)

- Climate change threatens drinking water reserves. Flooded residential areas, pestilences, millions of refugees – the ocean level will rise as a result of global warming. A totally unconsidered aspect: Penetrating saltwater lessens drinking water reserves. (Spiegel Online, Nov. 7, 2007)

- Alarming report: UN climate experts point out terrifying scenarios. Glaciers could melt; animal and plant species could die out. Rising temperatures bring the threat of floods, droughts and more infectious diseases: The UN climate report released today draws a gloomy picture. Global warming can no longer be stopped – at best it can be slowed down. (Spiegel Online, Nov. 11, 2007)

- Climate Crash 2035: The world is running away. The Intergovernmental Panel on Climate Change's (IPCC) forecast for the earth: melting polar caps, devastating storms, droughts and diluvial floods. Millions of people could become climate refugees. (Bild am Sonntag, Dec. 2, 2007)

- Climate Study: Number of flood victims will triple by 2070. (Welt Online, Dec. 4, 2007)

- Review: 2007 – more disastrous than ever. Storm tides, forest fires, strong earthquakes: Never before were there so many disasters as in 2007 – one insurance company counted almost 1000 natural disasters. The damage caused can hardly be estimated. (Spiegel Online, Dec. 31, 2007)

- Natural disasters doubled by climate change. Famines, droughts, melting glaciers – The climate change is evident and according to experts, even irreversible. (Welt Online, Jan. 21, 2008)

- Researchers warn of climate famines.
  In circa 20 years, the climate change could already plunge whole regions into famine. Impending water shortage is predicted for western USA. (Spiegel Online, Feb. 1, 2008)

- The pestilence "man" has attacked the world's oceans.
  Not only the oil slicks caused by tanker accidents and industrial waste water discharged into the oceans, but also over-fishing and the consequences of the climate change appear to be finishing off the oceans. (Spiegel Online, Feb. 15, 2008)

- Warning from the UN: Glaciers melting at record tempo. (Spiegel Online, Mar. 16, 2008)

- Greenpeace expects 200 million climate refugees. Climate expert Karsten Smid warns of humanitarian disaster. (German Radio, Apr. 2, 2008)

"How can God let disasters, earth upheavals and dying happen? Why doesn't God intervene?" is surely something many a reader asks himself.

In this book, we want to point out that God does not send disasters to humankind – on the contrary: God has given warning in time!

At all times, God has spoken through righteous men and women, through His prophets. God, the Eternal, even sent His Son, Christ, the Co-Regent of the heavens, to this earth.

God admonished; He gave warning and showed His children the way back to their divine origin.

Many may know the words of Isaiah:
The earth shall be utterly empty and utterly plundered; for the LORD has spoken this word. The earth mourns and withers; the world languishes and withers; the highest people of the earth languish. The earth lies defiled under its inhabitants; for they have transgressed the laws, violated the statutes, broken the everlasting covenant. (Is. 24:3-5)

Or the warning words of Jesus of Nazareth:
And when you hear of wars and tumults, do not be terrified, for these things must first take place, but the end will not be at once. Then he said to them: Nation will rise against nation, and kingdom against kingdom. There will be great earthquakes, and in various places, famines and pestilences. And there will be terrors and great signs from heaven. (Lk. 21:9-11)

During this time, God has again sent a great prophet to the people, Gabriele, the prophetess and messenger of God for our time, through whom He unmistakably announced and still announces worldwide His message and warnings to humankind. But the majority of people, above all, the caste of priests, who were against the prophets at all times, did not and do not listen to the word of God.
Now the apocalyptic time has begun.

The Law of Cause and Effect

It was a clever move on the part of the church institutions to withhold from their faithful the law of cause and effect, of sowing and reaping. With this, the cornerstone was laid for the so-called "mysteries of God" and the "unfathomable will of God." For the dissemination of such a teaching, learned theologians were, of course, needed. With rhetorical skill and the practice of ritual acts, they were able to make people believe that intermediaries are necessary to appease God for so long, that most people actually ended up giving financial support to these institution for centuries. However, at the present, belief in the institutions of the church is dwindling more and more, because many people are realizing that the sinking ship of the world cannot be saved, not even by church dignitaries.

How empty the doctrines of the theologians are became particularly clear after the great Tsunami disaster on Dec. 26, 2004, which may have been the greatest natural disaster in the history of humankind. The question now became inevitable: "Where is God? How could God allow this?" This is a question for which the church does have a term – it is the so-called "theodicy question" – but a satisfactory answer can be found neither in the Protestant nor the Vatican Church.

The following answers were offered by the Vatican Church, for instance: The Austrian Catholic Cardinal Christoph Schoenborn gave a speech on Jan. 19, 2005, with, among others, the following words: *I don't know if there really is an answer to this question: Why the suffering? Often remaining silent, a quiet compassion, is the only fitting attitude when faced with great suffering.*[1] The Swiss Roman Catholic Bishop Amédée Grab posed the following question during the course of a memorial service: *Why are you sleeping, Lord God? Why are you concealing your face, why do you forget our misfortune?* And the German Cardinal Wetter came to the conclusion: *... we will not find an answer to the question of why. We had to learn painfully that we do not live in paradise.* And Radio Vatican released the following comment on Dec. 28, 2004: *According to the opinion of the dogmatist Bernd Jochen Hilberath of Tübingen, Germany, disasters put theology in a position of having no explanation. ... Answers to the question of how God could allow disasters have always been unsatisfactory in the past.*

Theology's inability to give an explanation was shown not only in the answers of the past, but also of the present, as was clearly demonstrated by the quotes from Catholic theologians presented above.

But not only the Vatican Church struggled to find answers, the theologians of the Lutheran Church were also helpless. The Praeses of the Association of Protestant-Lutheran Churches in Rhineland, Germany, Nikolaus Schneider, emphasized that he has *no theological-dogmatic answer on the will of God in the midst of the rage of death.* Schneider's explanation: *God does not play with his creation. However, his creation is not perfect.*[2] And according to the opinion of theology Professor Werner Klän of the Lutheran Theological University in Oberursel, in the Taunus (region of Germany), there is no general answer to the question: "Where was God when the flood came?" It is *a question that cannot be answered,* he said, and indicated that when in doubt, help can be found in the *indiscernibility of God.*[3] And the

13

"Lutheran Press Service" published on Dec. 28, 2004 the views of the theologian Hans Gerhard Behringer, as follows: *... The question "Why does God allow this?" according to Behringer can be answered only with difficulty. People ask themselves the "why" question when life becomes fragile. A part of human maturity is to learn to live with unanswerable questions.* It is actually amazing that adults are satisfied with such answers and are also willing to pay church taxes for them! But this theologian only sticks valiantly to Luther, the founder of his church. Because for Luther the question about the "why" concerning misfortune or well-being was the worst kind of diabolical temptation. Luther said: *The worst challenges to our faith are when the devil brings us to look for the causes of well-being and misfortune ... The "why" has tormented all saints.[4]* And so, Luther's adherents must learn to live with unanswered questions, because the question of why, that is, the application of logical interpretation, is, according to him, a diabolical temptation!

Aside from the "mysteries of God," the Vatican Church introduced an argument that can be applicable to everything, namely: "Credo quia absurdum," which means "I believe because it is absurd." This motto also became clear in the theological-spiritual commentary by Father Eberhard von Gemmingen broadcast by Radio Vatican on Dec. 29, 2004:

Of course, after such a natural disaster, even for believing people, questions come up: Where is God? How can he allow this? Isn't he almighty? Can't he prevent such things? Or is he almighty and doesn't want to prevent them? How can he allow nature to commit such murder? No wonder that such questions come up ...[5]

The question: "How can God allow nature to commit such murder?" is interesting. With murder, we understand premeditated killing under circumstances that reveal a particular reprehensibleness in the basic attitude of the culprit. Since according to this statement, nature murdered only with the permission of God, then according to the Vatican statement God must be the culprit, who acted from a particularly reprehensible disposition.?! This may be Catholic, but it has nothing to do with Christ and with the true God! Or is the Vatican Church here addressing its own behavior patterns, which it has practiced against people, animals and nature throughout all the centuries? A statement by the renowned church historian Karlheinz Deschner characterizes this church as follows:

After intensely studying the history of Christianity, I know of no organization in antiquity, the Middle Ages and present times, including and especially the 20th century, that at the same time is so long, so continuously and so terribly burdened with crime as is the Christian Church, most particularly the Roman Catholic Church.[6]

But let's continue to read what Father Eberhard von Gemmingen had to say:

Such disasters can remind us that we can't take a look at God's cards, that his deeds are a secret, a mystery, sometimes a very painful mystery. ... If we think we understand God, that is an illusion. We cannot understand; we can only trust that behind all this is a meaning that we will someday recognize in His bright light. But today, we remain in the dark.

If the theologians want to remain in the dark, that is their decision. However, to every alert person with a heart and a mind, it does point out where the theologians are leading him. But there is a way out of this, which is expressed very clearly in the Revelation of John. There it says: *Come out of her, my people, lest you take part in her sins, lest you share in her plagues.* (Rev. 18:4)

The Catholic theologian talks about mysteries of God that can be very painful. But isn't it much more painful when theologians, who call themselves Christians, claim that God has secrets? God, the Eternal, does not need secrets, but those who adorn themselves with having studied God do; and yet, they know less about Him, or know Him even less than many a simple man of the people.

Could it be that "mysteries of God," which the churches like to talk about so much, could also be described as a white lie? Perhaps it is a sham, to cover up the falsifications of the teachings of Jesus by theologians. The most successful step in this direction was taken at the Second Council of Constantinople in the year 553, where the teaching of reincarnation disappeared from the teachings of the Church by way of a majority ruling.[7] With this, they also eliminated the law of cause and effect, of sowing and reaping, even though it can literally still be found in the Bible. In the Letter to the Galatians, it says: *Do not be deceived; God is not mocked, for whatever a man sows, that he will also reap.* (Gal. 6:7)

If the theologians had not suppressed the knowledge about this spiritual law, then so many people would not have been helplessly at the mercy of their fate; they could have understood it and overcome it. Then many could have made use of the chance, by way of gaining insight and changing their ways, to develop independence and security in themselves and to find their way to a higher quality of life.

Since the law of cause and effect is of major significance for us humans, it was explained to us by Christ already in the first divine revelations given via Gabriele. In the year 1980, He said:

What is the meaning of "cause and effect" or "we will reap what we sow"? Oh see! "For every action there is a reaction," so says man. Nevertheless, he cannot comprehend these causalities and effects. In this hour, I want to give you an understanding of the causalities of humankind that take place on this earth.

My dear children, you should now imagine your dwelling planet, your earth, as a large person! Let us call him the earth-man. I have already explained the individual organs. Now, among other things, I will talk about the garment of the great earth-man. The garment consists of the kingdoms of the minerals, of nature and of the animals. The magnetic fields of the earth-man are the nerve centers, the magnetic currents, the pathways of the nerves. What do you have? Your garment of the moment is also from the substance of the earth, that is, water and earth.

Oh see! The eternal life of God streams through all life forms, through the organs of the earth-man, through the garment. When man now acts against this earth-man, at the same time he is acting against his own life. If man only knew that as soon as he violates an animal, he is harming his own body, by shadowing his soul and reducing the inner strength, the spirit-power! The unknowing person steps and acts thoughtlessly on this great earth-man! He intentionally and unintentionally destroys the kingdom of nature and the animal kingdom! Oh see! Animals are bred for slaughter. The thoughts that precede this already include the unlawful word "death" – kill for meat! Man acts against the great law of God. He acts against the commandment "You shall not kill!"

This also holds true for the great earth-man, for the earth. Everything that is done willfully penetrates your soul and burdens it. And so, humanity is constantly destroying this earth! He damages the great earth-man and does not think about the fact that one day this great earth-man will defend itself ...

Dear readers, today we already have to experience how the great earth-man is defending himself! In His revelation, Christ continued:

... so you people will ask: How should we know that when we damage the earth, the effect falls back on us? We were not told, "do not damage the earth," but "take what the earth gives you!"

Do you actually take what the earth gives you? Do you not strive over and over again to draw still more from the earth?

Verily, I say to you: You humans have not yet grasped that the more you want to take from the earth, the less it will give you in times to come, because you are changing the inner life and thus the constellation. You are the perpetrators of this coming event.

Only the fewest of people recognize what is coming. And when they hear about it, they think of God, the punishing and wrathful God. Oh no! What you sow, you will reap – unless you turn back! ...

Clear words that Christ spoke to us back then! The perpetrator of the coming events is not a punishing God, but man. At that time, in 1980, many people on the earth still could have turned back and changed their ways and thus, many a thing could have been turned to the good. During the following years, the divine world spoke to us human beings through Gabriele again and again about the causal law, the law of cause and effect. In 1986, for example, Brother Emanuel, the cherub of divine wisdom, explained to us again through Gabriele:

Dear friends, every action is followed by a reaction. Many people ask how the future will be, that is, what will happen in the future.

Much has been prophesied. The words in the Bible also tell some things, for Jesus already spoke about the coming time. Many listen to the news media; they read newspapers and magazines and learn what is taking place in this world. And as already revealed, they think more or less about what the future will bring. Dear friends, what will the future bring? Jesus of Nazareth said it: The future brings what human beings have sown during past epochs and in this epoch.

The Insult "End-time Apostle." Theologians Are No Longer Scoffing Today

The Church soon noticed that the teaching of the Spirit of God through Gabriele, the prophetess and messenger of God, is just as revolutionary as were the words of Jesus of Nazareth 2000 years ago. The teaching of God is ingenious and clear and so simple in its logic that no intermediary is needed. Original Christianity has no priests. It is not based on a human being, but solely on Jesus, the Christ, the great Spirit of infinity, who dwells in each one of us. No person can lead another person to God, our Father; only Christ can do this. The path to God is the Inner Path, because God does not dwell in temples of stone; every person can experience Him only within himself. No priests, no excellencies, eminencies, pastors and however else they may call themselves, are needed for this path, but there is someone who shows us the way; it is Gabriele, the prophetess and messenger of God. She is a role model for the people, but each person can walk this path only for himself.

This fact alone poses a great threat to the power-institution called church. This is why they sent their agents of defamation, to do to the prophetess of the present time what they have done to all enlightened men and women.

In the year 1980, Christ spoke:

As I said at the beginning of My words: The Spirit tries over and over again to reveal to humankind the all-encompassing truths of the heavens. But humankind has silenced God by affirming the persecution and killing of the prophets, also called proclaimers.

Once again, the Spirit of God tries to move you people to change your ways...

20

The Spirit of God tried this at all times by warning people of their causes, which they would meet as effects if they did not change themselves in time. But the theologians behaved as they always did. Since it is no longer in keeping with the times to burn people at the stake these days, and it is thus no longer possible to eliminate a prophet by murdering him, they try to silence the prophetess of God through character assassination and ridicule. The one who believed in the word of God was ridiculed as an "end-time apostle."

Nine years later, (1989) after the Spirit of God had warned humankind with numerous revelations through the mouth of a prophet, the spiritual teacher Brother Emanuel said:

At all times, the Spirit of God has given warning, and Christ, your Redeemer, and the messengers of light have admonished.

Then he spoke about our sister Gabriele:

Many years ago, when our sister received the inner word, the eternal Spirit addressed the theologians.

Letters were sent to bishops and to the so-called "pope," who heads the Catholic side. Christ admonished; Christ gave warning; Christ pointed out the weaknesses. Through the mouth of a prophet, through His instrument, Christ called for people to change their ways and spoke of the coming times. He asked humankind to turn back and change its ways. He asked the theologians, the bishops, the so-called pope, to strive for a Christian life and not a human one. What was the response? Jeering, mockery, derision, ridicule and much more – right up until this very day.

Two years later, in 1991, Christ took up this topic again. But now, since the people had not wanted to listen to the word of

God, another time had begun. The hands on the great cosmic clock had moved forward. Christ spoke:

Many years ago I admonished again through My instrument. Particularly those who were and are in the Christian religions and call themselves Christian accused those who spoke of the so-called end-time, saying: "They are so-called end-time apostles, who want to stir up the people, and build up an external power structure through fear and the like."

Who was servile to them? He will be with them today.
My children all over the world: There is no going back! The floods are rising. The conflagrations are growing ever larger. Famine, disasters, wars and the like are coming one after the other. Which land will be spared? The land that is the inner kingdom.

From year to year, it became clearer that the Spirit of God was by no means creating panic, but has only been providentially warning the people, His children, in time, to keep them from calamity. For several years now, however, we no longer hear laughing from the side of the theologians; for now, even the scientists are confirming what the Spirit of God had already revealed through the mouth of a prophet.
The man-made climate change and its disastrous consequences are becoming a topic of discussion in the media more and more. The church has recognized the trend and now the officials of the church institutions are attempting to jump on the train that actually pulled out long ago. They are doing this by suddenly pretending to be protectors of the climate: Papers are being written, conversations held and alliances made. But in reality it was and ultimately is, the leaders of the church who bear the responsibility for the impending

climate disaster. For they were the ones who ridiculed the warnings given by the Spirit of God and trampled upon them.

Infectious Diseases and Pestilences

Jesus of Nazareth announced a change of times already 2000 years ago. This can still be read in the Bible today, for example, where it says:

Then he said to them, "Nation will rise against nation, and kingdom against kingdom. There will be great earthquakes, and in various places famines and pestilences. And there will be terrors and great signs from heaven." (Lk. 21:10-11)

Christ referred to these statements in 1988, when He said the following through Gabriele:

As Jesus of Nazareth, I announced the great change of times, the disasters and much more: One nation will be against another; pestilences, famine, diseases and epidemics will come; but the page has not turned completely. Wars and much more, earth disasters and the like will turn the page, and then the inner kingdom, the Kingdom of Peace on this earth, will shine.

In this book, we will address the individual topics in more detail. We would like to start with diseases and epidemics, which have continued to gain ground during recent years. Christ often warned about this through Gabriele. For example, He said in 1991:

For that which I indicated as Jesus of Nazareth, is breaking in over humankind <u>now</u> – wars, natural disasters, civil wars, hunger, need, suffering, misery, diseases and much more. Yes, the polluted earth is rebelling and swallowing up many.

And in 1992, Christ pointed out the following:
Look into your world and recognize that the blows of fate, the diseases, hardships, epidemics, disasters are increasing more and more. And so, this means that the earth is shaking itself. It is lying in fever and spews forth everything that does not belong to the innermost part of the earth, to the pure Being.

You can deduce from the following facts the course of development of infectious diseases and epidemics:

• Epidemics and infectious diseases are the primary cause of death worldwide. 17 million people die annually as the result of an infection. The greatest killers are tuberculosis, AIDS and malaria.[8]

• Since 1980, 35 new infectious diseases have appeared – so many as never before in such a short time.[9]

• The World Health Organization (WHO) estimates that approximately one third of the world population is infected with tuberculosis. Meanwhile tuberculosis heads the list worldwide in the statistics of infectious diseases. According to WHO, particularly alarming is the development of resistance in the tuberculosis pathogen. Every year half a million new cases develop through multi-resistant pathogens against which the antibiotics usually used to treat tuberculosis are no longer effective. An especially dangerous variety, which is resistant to nearly all antibiotics, has meanwhile spread in 45 countries.[10]

- The plague has not been exterminated by far. WHO registers between 1000 and 3000 cases annually. A research group has published an appeal warning of extensive new outbreaks of the plague; the number of observed cases is again increasing in several regions. Not lastly, the researchers are alarmed by the resistance to antibiotics.[11]

- With circa 100 million cases per year and 25,000 deaths, worldwide, Dengue fever is the disease most transmitted by mosquitoes, (*Aedes aegypti* rarely *Aedes albopictus*) and it is spreading rapidly. Its increased appearance in South America and South East Asia is all the more unsettling, because there is almost no means of fighting it effectively.[12]

- 1.5 to 2.7 million people die annually of malaria, circa half of them are children under five years of age. The number of new cases annually is estimated at 300 to 500 million.[13]

- 11,000 people become infected with AIDS every day; 8000 die from it every day. Since the discovery of the AIDS virus in 1981, 25 million victims were counted up until 2005. 88 million will become infected during the next 10 years. 33 million people live with AIDS; about 2.1 million are children under 15. Young people between 15 and 24 make up 40% of all people newly infected with HIV.[14]

- Hepatitis is developing into a treacherous epidemic. Above all, hepatitis C is a chronic illness of epidemic-like proportions. 400 million people worldwide are suffering from this illness; in Germany approximately 800,000 people have been hit by it. Hepatitis C is one of the ten most frequent causes of death in Germany today.[15]

- In 2008, WHO made it known that presently 150,000 people are already dying annually due to climate-related diseases and injuries.[16] During the extremely hot summer in 2003, there were more than 70,000 victims in Europe alone.

Climate Change

The divine world not only warned of the increased appearance of epidemics and diseases, but often pointed out further changes involving earth upheavals. Already in 1980 the spiritual world spoke through Gabriele:

Changes in the poles and spring tides are mentioned again and again. I say to you: There will be a colossal change in the poles and unending suffering will break in over this earth: illnesses that the earth and humankind have never before witnessed. The oceans will seek new basins and your beautiful valleys will be the basins for the water. ...

What was still unimaginable for many people in 1980 is becoming more and more visible today. The polar caps are melting; spring tides are increasing and scientists are warning of an extreme rise in ocean levels.

26

The question of whether man changes the climate has long been answered with "yes" by international climate research. The global climate change is in full swing, and its signs are unmistakable.

- Man must reckon with a disaster today four times more often than 20 years ago. While in the early 1980s, circa 120 natural disasters were counted per year, such as drought, floods and storms, this number is currently about 500! According to the result of a study by the British aid organization Oxfam, a rising number of disasters are to be expected in the future. Oxfam names the global climate change as the primary reason for this massive increase. But it is not only the number of environmental disasters that is rising, but also their intensity and the number of people affected will continue to increase. Since the mid-1980s, they have risen almost 70%.[17]

The divine world gave warning in time. For example, in 1984 Christ pointed out the following:

The future of humankind is written in the atmosphere. The earth and the oceans also bear witness to what man has sown. Verily, verily, I say to you: The time is near when the waters will take many people away, when the planet Earth will rebel and swallow up everything that it can get hold of. And it will be that the waters will cleanse many parts of the earth. And different climatic conditions will appear. ...

And two years later – in 1986 – a high spirit being from the heavens, named Brother Emanuel, explained through Gabriele:

Atomic power pollutes not only the oceans, rivers, lakes and the earth. Atomic power heats up the oceans; the polar caps begin to melt. For your better understanding: The oceans are the stove; the earth is the burner on the stove. The oceans are heated up, the burner begins to glow. All these negative vibrations have their effect on souls and human beings; earthquakes, volcanic eruptions and the like are the so-called natural disasters. But the disasters also continue among the people. The climate is changing; the people are heated up; the nervous system becomes tense. Everything that a person has stored in his consciousness and subconscious and in his soul garments takes its effect. And what happens on the earth? Murder, hostility, rivalries, civil wars ...

The melting of the polar caps and the warming of the oceans, which the divine world warned about already during the 1980s, is a dramatic reality today:

- The Artic is melting faster than the climate models up to now predicted. In the summer of 2007, melting of the Artic reached its interim highpoint: In September, 23% less ice floes were registered than in the previous record low. In 2008, data from NASA showed that the percentage of the two to five year-old permanent ice sank from 40% in the winter of 2006-2007 to 30% in the winter of 2007-2008. The lost ice surface in the Artic is 1.5 times as large as Alaska.

  US-NASA climate researcher Jay Zwally predicted: "At this rate, the Arctic Ocean could be nearly ice-free at the end of summer by 2012, much faster than earlier predictions."[18]

- In 2007, Greenland lost twice as much ice as exists in all of the Alps. Greenland's ice sheet is the greatest unknown in all climate models used until now to calculate the rise of ocean levels. A US research group under Bea Csatho of the Geology Department at the University of Buffalo released a study in the "Journal of Glaciology," which precisely explored for the first time the melting activity and the dynamics of the Greenland glacier. Its conclusions are alarming: It estimated that ocean levels would rise 36 to 118 centimeters by the end of the century; this is double as much as has been predicted till now by the IPCC. And this is only the number for the global average! According to changes in ocean currents and movement of continental plates, it could come to local rises of several meters. There is enough ice in Greenland to cause ocean levels to rise almost seven meters in an extreme case scenario.[19]

A few days after these facts were made known by the American research group, scientists from the British Proudman Oceanographic Laboratory announced that the sea level could rise up to 1.5 meters by 2100. This is three times as much as what was predicted by the IPCC in 2007. If the calculations by the researchers are accurate, then in 2100 circa 90% of the densely populated country of Bangladesh will be flooded. Africa and Asia would be hit hardest by a higher sea level. The Republic of China would have to resettle circa 72 million people.

- With a rise of one meter circa 14,000 square kilometers of coastline and backcountry on the North Sea and Baltic Sea would lie under the waterline in Germany. This represents about 4% of the total land surface and an area in which over three million German citizens live. A further result of the rising water levels: Storm surges would penetrate further inland.[20]

* Without countermeasures – insofar as such things can, at all, promise permanent success – with a rise in ocean levels of one meter worldwide, 150,000 square kilometers of land surface would be permanently flooded, of which 62,000 square kilometers would be coastal wetlands. 180 million people would be affected and damages of 1.1 trillion dollars could be expected, based on today's population and property ownership.[21]

* The mighty ice sheet of the Antarctic is the largest ice reservoir on earth with up to 4000 meters thickness. But now, global warming is causing the ice to begin to thaw, even in the "freezer chest" of our planet. Scientists estimate that the West Antarctic Ice Sheet lost about 132 billion tons of ice in 2006, compared to a loss of 83 billion tons in 1996. In addition, the Antarctic Peninsula lost about 60 billion tons of ice in 2006. This amount demonstrates that the melting of the Antarctic glacier has clearly accelerated during the last ten years. A satellite survey between 1996 and 2006 found that the net loss of ice from Antarctica rose by about 75%, as the movement of glaciers towards the sea speeded up. "To put these figures into perspective, 4 billion tons of ice is enough to provide drinking water for the whole UK population for one year," said Professor Jonathan Bamber, of the University of Bristol. "We think the glaciers of the Antarctic are moving faster toward the sea. The computer models of a future sea-level rise have not really taken this into account."

The melting and breaking off of ice blocks in the Antarctic contributes to the rise of ocean levels, because the ice also slides from the land into the ocean. For years, scientists have observed an increasing rate of melting at certain points of the continent.[22]

- Scientists suspect that aside from global warming, a volcano under the ice sheet of Western Antarctica is contributing to the strongly increased melting of glacial ice. Its eruption took place circa 2000 years ago; however, it is still active. [23]

- According to research by Professor Wilfried Korth of the Berlin University of Applied Sciences, the Greenland ice sheet is losing up to 150,000 tons of ice every year – a result of global warming. In the summer of 2007, the smallest expansion and thickness of the arctic sea ice until now was determined.

  The changes in the surface of the ice have been known for some time, but now the thickness has also been measured and shows a clear decrease from 2.5 meters in 1998 to one meter in September 2007.[24]

- A German-Danish research team has determined that the water in the North Sea and the Baltic Sea is getting warmer and warmer. In the period from 1985 to 2000, the mean temperature of the water has risen 1.4 degrees in the months of July-September. This rise is three times as high as that predicted by the IPCC report.[25]

In 1986 Brother Emanuel compared the earth to a "stove burner"; five years later, he said through Gabriele:

Recognize that through man's causes the earth has become a fiery oven. Layers of the atmosphere are dissolving – the world is like a pressure cooker standing on the earth; it is boiling. ... So recognize that the deserts are still expanding, but when the waters come ...

Dear brothers and sisters, mere highlights of the future, which in reality are already the present – for much is withheld from you. ...

This tactic of withholding the facts is just as common today as in 1989. An example of this is, for instance, the alarming report of the Nobel-Prize winning IPCC, which was published in 2007 stimulating great interest from the media and the public. The report's conclusion: The climate change conditions are indeed very dramatic, but could still be prevented. However, in April 2008, the voices of climatologists became loud, accusing the panel of foul play: The assumption that the dangerous climate change could still be prevented with the measures suggested is wrong and outdated. And instead of telling the public the plain truth, namely, that humankind has already reached the threshold of a climate collapse or even gone beyond it, sand was more or less thrown in the public's eyes by the panel. What can we still rely on? [26]

Even though the divine world never gives years, it is certain that what is conveyed to us in messages from the All is in store for us human beings. In another message through Gabriele in 1991, for example, God-Father pointed out events of the future with the following words:

What Jesus of Nazareth revealed will continue to occur on the earth. The nations will fight each other. Civil wars, pestilences, diseases, miseries and troubles, the homeless and the dead and much more will be on the earth. The good friend, who has become the enemy of man, will again shake off all that is on and in the earth and in the waters – and the sun and the stars will do what is to be done through an atmosphere riddled with holes. ...

Today, science can no longer withhold the upheavals taking place on the earth, for the effects are not only visible to many people, but tangible, as well.

* The International Strategy for Disaster Reduction (ISDR), a branch of the UN, registered (until Feb. 2006) a sharp rise in hydrometeorological disasters. In 1970, there were circa 30 disastrous floods worldwide, but meanwhile, it has climbed to 130 floods annually. It is similar with storms. Hydrometeorological disasters, which include landslides and droughts, presently trigger more than three fourths of all natural disasters.[27]

* According to the Red Cross, the number of natural disasters caused by the climate change has doubled during the past 20 years. Circa 400 severe floods, storms and heat waves have taken place per year. During the 1980s, Red Cross experts counted circa 200 climate-related natural disasters per year.[28]

Brother Emanuel said that the world is like a pressure cooker that is standing on a boiling-hot earth. Recent years have clearly confirmed this: 2001 and 2002 were unusually hot and the summer of 2003 broke all records in Europe.[29] In 2006, scientists at NASA's Goddard Institute for Space Studies reported that earth temperatures have reached their highest levels in the past 12,000 years. According to a NASA study, 2005 was the warmest year ever registered, and 2006 and 2007 set many weather records. The global mean temperature of the earth has risen circa 0.8°C, of which 0.6°C occurred during the past 30 years.[30]

Let us remember the words of Christ in 1984: *"The future of humankind is written in the atmosphere"* and the words of our spiritual teacher, Brother Emanuel, from 1989: *"Layers of the atmosphere are dissolving."*
And in 1991, God-Father spoke of *"an atmosphere riddled with holes."* Today everyone knows what was meant by this, for the ozone hole and the consequences resulting from it have now been scientifically determined. A few facts concerning this:

- Ozone concentrations are becoming a worldwide problem. Above all, in several regions of Africa, the ozone levels have doubled within two years. The worldwide increasing consumption of energy is leading to a large-scale increase of ozone, thus globally lowering the quality of air. Often ozone from concentrated industrial centers like Southeast Asia is transported halfway around the world and contributes to air pollution in Brazil, for instance.[31]

- NASA scientists reported that on Sept. 24, 2006 the area of the ozone hole over the Antarctic exceeded 29 million km^2. This represents an area approximately the size of the USA and Russia together. Another negative record in parameter concentration was reached on Oct. 8, 2006. At that time, nearly all the ozone in the layers between 13 and 21 kilometers above the Antarctic had been destroyed.[32]

A result of global warming is, among other things, flooding. In the following, several facts regarding this are presented.

- According to the estimate of experts at the United Nations University, one billion people, one sixth of the present world population, are threatened with the danger of flooding and hundred-year floods.[33]

- According to a UN report, there were particularly many floods in 2007. The number of floods was far higher than the sum of all other natural disasters put together. On the whole, there were 20% more floods than the average of the previous seven years.[34]

- *The impact of climate change and urban development could more than triple the number of people around the world exposed to coastal flooding by 2070, according to a new report by the OECD* [Organization for Economic Cooperation and Development], *co-authored by experts from academia and the private sector.*
  Ranking port cities with high exposure and vulnerability to climate extremes finds that around 150 million people could be exposed to a 1-in-100 year coastal flood event by 2070, up from 40 million today.
  The experts assume a rise in ocean levels of half a meter during the next 60 years. *Around half of the total population exposure to coastal flooding caused by storm surge and damage from high winds is contained in just ten cities today. ... Over the coming decades, the unprecedented growth and development of the Asian mega-cities will be a key factor in driving the increase of coastal flood risk globally.*[35]

- Two thirds of the largest metropolises such as New York, Tokyo or Shanghai are located in areas directly threatened by the climate change. This is shown by study maps produced by the International Institute for the Environment and Development. Only huge investment and resettlement could prevent flood and storm disasters. The researchers calculated that in the year 2000 circa 634 million people lived in the endangered coastal mega cities, three fourths of them in Asia. Especially endangered are the coastal regions in poor countries.[36]

- Meanwhile there are no longer grounds to doubt that human beings cause the warming of the oceans. Oceanographers of the Scripps Institute at the University of California in San Diego have substantiated that various computer simulations agree almost 100% with the factual warming of the oceans.[37]

- At the same time, the saline content of the oceans is changing because of increasing melt water. More than 20,000 cubic kilometers of freshwater from melting polar ice has poured into the Atlantic between 1965 and 1995. The decreased salinity of the Atlantic waters endangers the North Atlantic Current. This current pushes the seawater from the far north into depths in the southern hemisphere like a conveyor belt, and then back up to the surface. The North Atlantic Current significantly influences the climate in northern and central Europe.[38]

- During the past years, the oceans have become more and more salty at the equator. The climatic warming causes a strong evaporation in the tropical oceans, while at the same time causing stronger precipitation in the Polar Regions contributing to a thinning of the seawater. It is probable that this change in salinity will cause considerable changes in deep-water currents of the oceans, which, in turn, influence the climate.[39]

- Glaciers are melting at record speed: A study by the World Glacier Monitoring Service (University of Zurich, Geography Department) demonstrated that between 2004/ 2005 and 2005/2006, glaciers melted approximately twice as fast as during the previous two decades. While during the 1980s and up to the turn of the millennium, they lost an average of 30 cm thickness per year, since 2000 they have lost half a meter annually and during recent years even 70 cm. According to statements made by the scientists, these figures are part of an accelerating trend for which there is no prospect of an end. The glaciers are natural water reserves, which millions or even billions of people depend upon.[40]

- Permafrost occurs in Arctic and Antarctic regions as well as in high mountains worldwide. Globally, nearly a quarter of all land area is permafrost, whereby most of it – circa 23 million km^2 – is in the northern hemisphere. Huge amounts of carbon reserves are stored in the permafrost, far more than formerly assumed. When the permafrost melts, methane and CO_2 will be released into the atmosphere. With increasing global warming, an increased release of greenhouse gases could result from this source. The release of just a fragment of the carbon stored in artic soils would be sufficient to tangibly raise the concentration of atmospheric greenhouse gases. On the other hand, the climate change already underway could cause underwater continental slopes, presently stabilized by methane hydrate, to begin to slide: by changing an ocean current, for instance. Such an event apparently led to a global climate collapse 55 million years ago, with fatal results for many species of living beings.[41]

- For years, scientists have observed with concern how, due to the warming of the earth in summer, large parts of Siberia are being transformed from a frosty landscape into shallow bodies of water. In 2006, an international research group determined that 3.8 million tons of methane are released annually by this thawing permafrost soil. Even though this share is still small when compared to total methane emissions, it could rapidly increase, because it is part of a vicious circle: The more methane in the air, the warmer it becomes. And so, the land continues to thaw, and even more methane ends up in the atmosphere.[42]

- Russian polar scientists have strong evidence that the first stages of melting are underway. They've studied the largest shelf sea in the world, off the coast of Siberia, where the Asian continental shelf stretches across an underwater area six times the size of Germany, before falling off gently into the Arctic Ocean. In the permafrost bottom of the 200-meter-deep sea, enormous stores of gas hydrates lie dormant in mighty frozen layers of sediment.
The carbon content of the ice-and-methane mixture is estimated at 540 billion tons. If all the stored gas escapes, scientists believe the methane content of the planet's atmosphere would increase twelve fold. "The result would be a catastrophic global warming," say the scientists.[43]

- Over 50% of the plant and animal species could soon disappear from our earth, if the climate should continue to warm up, as predicted. Scientists warned of this in a study published in the "Proceedings of the Royal Society B" in 2007.[44]

- The greenhouse CO_2 gas is also damaging the organisms of the oceans. Increased CO_2 levels raise the pressure in the atmosphere causing the gas to be increasingly dissolved in seawater. This, in turn, decreases the PH level and the ocean becomes acidic. The external skeletons of sea organisms, which consist of calcium carbonate, are thus partially dissolved in surface waters. Particularly affected are organisms like coral and plankton.[45]

- Studies show that even a moderate rise in temperature is sufficient to trigger a "positive feedback," which leads to an acceleration of the climate change. The resulting over-proportional warming process can cause the entire eco-system to tip over.

Until now climate researchers have identified 15 such tipping points. On the other hand, a reset-mechanism to stop the warming has not been found. If only the positive feedbacks become active, the results will be fatal. According-ing to experts at the Potsdam Institute for Climate Impact Research: The earth-system would go into a "warm operating status" that would last at least 10,000 years. Whole regions could become uninhabitable. Their inhabitants would have to flee to the last cool refuges in the polar regions. Then our whole civilization could hang in the balance.[46]

These are several facts that demonstrate the consequences of the climate change, of which God gave warning in time. However, the Spirit of the Christ of God not only indicated the destruction of the atmosphere, but also described the world as a pressure cooker standing on the earth and boiling. And so, it is not only the atmosphere that is contributing to global warming, but the innermost part of the earth is also heating up, as Christ explained to us in 1993:

You always think only of the atmosphere that is destroyed. But I say to you: The magma is heating up more and more and causing much to come into movement. The earth is heating up. The ice is melting. The floods are coming and the storms precede them. ...

We can deduce from the preceding facts how much the earth is heating up, the ice is melting and the floods are coming. But what do the measurements of the earth's temperature show?

- A study from July 2007 performed by German and Russian scientists, who have traveled regularly to the South Atlantic for almost four decades, shows that the coldest water, which is on the floor of the deep ocean there, is becoming ever warmer. The Antarctic bottom water is part of a global ocean circulation, which circulates water masses over a time scale of centuries. If these global circulations change, this will have a long-term effect on our climate.[47]

It remains to be seen whether scientists get on the track of the connection announced by the Spirit of God, or whether the results of the manmade climate change catch up with us before that.

What these consequences would look like and what will come to humankind was pointed out by God-Father to His human children in 1991, when He spoke through Gabriele:

What fate are many peoples and nations heading toward? The fate of destruction and devastation.

Jesus of Nazareth said what would come if the people did not turn back and change their ways. Have they turned back? They have made their greatest friend into an enemy – a friend who, since the beginning of humankind, has given humankind life, light and strength, a friend who nourished them, provided them with drink and offered them shelter, a home and food.

The friend was the planet earth with its atmosphere. What have people done to this friend, to the planet earth? They are poisoning nature. They are violating the entire earth. They are exploding the atmosphere; yes, they are wiping out life with bombs. The planet earth has to endure the most terrible substances. Many people care little whether the good friend suffers or whether it remains healthy. The good friend is sick! Yes, it is poisoned by chemical substances, by atomic tests, by the pollution of the waters and much more. It is so sick, the good friend, that it has now become the enemy of man.

And no nation can be victorious over this enemy. No nation can stamp it out and flatten it with bombs. No people can kill it – regardless of the weapons it uses. No person can butcher this enemy, trample it down or hurl it into squalor and horror. It is shaking itself – and what it brings forth is what the people have bombed into the good friend: destruction.

What Jesus of Nazareth revealed will continue to happen on the earth. Nations will fight each other. Civil wars,

41

pestilences, diseases, miseries and troubles, the homeless and the dead ones and much more will be on the earth. The good friend, who has become the enemy of man, will again shake off all that is on and in the earth and in the waters – and the sun and the stars will do what is to be done through an atmosphere riddled with holes. ...
And so, man has turned his good friend into a warring enemy, who is shaking off what was inflicted on him. For all causes are pressed to come into effect ...

We also find here the indication that God is not a punishing God who sends all kinds of disasters and tribulations to the people, but it is the people's causes that are pressing toward their effects. The planet earth was a good friend to us, but the human being has made it into a warlike enemy.

In several mighty revelations during the years 1996 and 1997, God-Father spoke up as plaintiff for the Mother Earth. His words were broadcast over numerous radio stations at that time and are partially published in books. In 1996, God-Father spoke the following (it can be read in "The Message from the All. The Prophecy of God Today. Not the Word of the Bible"):

Verily, verily, I say to you: I Am also the plaintiff for this earth, for the innocent creatures, for all life forms, for the animals, plants and minerals. ... The earth calls to Me, the Creator, for mercy, for freedom. ...
Verily, verily, I say to you: The vibrations of your negative behavior draw through the whole earth; they go into the atmosphere and come back to you. Who destroys the atmosphere – the God of love, who gave the earth a mantle so that you could live on the earth? But you – every single one of you – contribute to the fact that the mantle is

opening up and the forces of the universe are gradually burning you up ...

Just think of the summer of 2003. At that time we could experience to a certain extent what is meant that the forces of the universe are "gradually burning" us up. During this record summer, approximately 70,000 Europeans fell victim to the scorching heat. The earth calls to the Creator for mercy and freedom. For this reason, in 1997 God-Father said the following to us humans as plaintiff for the Mother Earth:

... And so, the last part of the Revelation of John, the Apocalypse, is gradually being fulfilled. And then there will be peace. How will this happen? Spoken in general terms for you humans – may the one who has ears to hear, hear. May the one who has eyes to see, see.
Mother Earth is shaking herself through the earthquakes. Mother Earth is shaking herself through the storms, through the forest fires and much more, and is calling: "You humans, what have you done to me? My children abuse and torture me. They torture the animals. Animals starve and die of thirst, for drought is advancing more and more, as dry as the hearts of the people." And Mother Earth calls: "My children what are you doing to me? What are you doing to the animals, to the plants and the minerals?" But the people listen just as little as they did to the prophets, to the true God, who I AM. They listened and listen just as little to Jesus, the Christ, their Redeemer. And Mother Earth is crying tear after tear, for the floods and the oceans are rising and she calls: "You children, what are you doing to me? I am unendingly sad over you. I can no longer carry you." And at all times, the people do not listen to the call of the tormented earth, to say

43

nothing of the word of God through the prophets, through spiritually enlightened men and women, through the fighters for the kingdom of the inner being. And so, the mouth of the earth, of Mother Earth, is opening up. It is the volcanoes. And Mother Earth calls: "I can no longer carry you now! – Peace, peace, peace," she calls. And the lava flows out of her mouth and covers great parts of the earth.

A part of this is the fact that your so-called satellites, the heavenly bodies you have created, will fall from your heavens, and there will be a great roar on this earth. Smaller and larger polar shifts will prepare for the big one, and there will be peace, for the earth's magma flows out and covers everything up."

The call of Mother Earth through the Creator was taken seriously by only a few people, and so today we are experiencing what God-Father spoke about in His revelation:

May the one who has ears to hear, hear. May the one who has eyes to see, see.

Storms

In His word to humankind in 1997, God-Father said that Mother Earth would shake herself through storms. But 1997 was not the first time that humankind was warned about this. Already in 1991, Christ said:

... and the atmosphere will give the signs of storm...

In 1993, Christ warned about what effects the signs of storm would have:

Oh see, the storms of the times are not only forecast – they are blowing, raging, on all continents. But this is only the beginning. Whole continents are beginning to wobble, because the earth plates are rotating more and more, since the earth's magma is heating up ever more. And so, the entire earth is also heating up. You always think only of the atmosphere that is destroyed. But I say to you: The magma is heating up more and more and causing much to come into movement. The earth is heating up. The ice is melting. The floods are coming and the storms precede them ...

I spoke of the storms of the times, which will afflict the earth. But recognize that violent storms will also sweep over the land and many a structure will collapse. The good soil will be taken from the fields. What you have planted will be torn from the fields, for the storms will rage violently and they will not only sweep over the land – they are like hurricanes that build up and cause whole towns, villages and cities to burst.

We were warned of this in 1993 – and now it has already become reality. A few scientific facts concerning this:

- Since 1970 storms and hail have claimed 909 lives in Germany. According to calculations by the Swiss reinsurer, Swiss Re, storm damages per year will rise by 2085 from 16 to 68%. The study says that three times as many damages for Germany are reckoned with than is the average in Europe. By 2085, the storm damages per year will more than double. Particularly severe "hurricanes of the century" will lose their special status, because they will occur every few decades. The reason for this is global warming, because it provides conditions favorable to the development of more storms. The intervals between severely damaging storms in Europe were recently less than ten years. And the most devastating storms occurred between 1990 and 2007.[48]

- More than 60 tornadoes were recorded in Germany in 2007. Three of them caused enormous damage during the hurricane "Kyrill" on Jan. 17, 2007. According to the meteorologist Thomas Sävert of the Meteomedia Storm Forecasting Center, the number of recorded tornadoes had risen drastically in the past several years. "Kyrill" was an unusual storm that raged over all of Germany. There was no place in Germany where it did not reach at least 100 kilometers per hour.[49]

- Due to the rising temperature in Europe, it must be assumed that the number as well as the intensity of European winter storms will increase considerably in the future. According to the storm report released by WWF in 2006, Great Britain and the Netherlands should prepare for strong hurricanes. Climate computer simulations calculate an increase of up to 25% more winter storms. The report says that the probability of severe storms in Germany, particularly on the coasts, will rise by 10%.[50]

- In 2007, hurricanes occurred in places that had never before experienced them, for example, Oman and Iran.[51] And for the first time, the Caribbean experienced two hurricanes of the maximum category 5. The tropical storm season lasted into December.[52]

- Since the 1970s, the intensity of tropical hurricanes has increased rapidly. The number of hurricanes of category 4 and 5 has nearly doubled. A study by Peter Webster of the Georgia Institute of Technology was released in 2005. In this analysis of hurricanes – known as typhoons or cyclones in other parts of the world – researchers counted 16 category 4 and 5 storms in the Atlantic-Caribbean-Gulf of Mexico between 1975 and 1989. In the eastern Pacific region, the increase was from 36 to 49 storms and from 85 to 116 in the western Pacific. In the southwest Pacific, the increase was from 10 to 22 powerful storms, while the total went from one to seven in the north Indian Ocean and from 23 to 50 in the south Indian Ocean.[53]

- The Atlantic hurricane season of 2005 was the most active season since consistent records have been kept, beginning in 1851. More than 28 tropical storms formed, of which 15 were hurricanes.
Hurricane Katrina: Circa 1800 people died. Particularly hard hit was the southern metropolis of New Orleans, which was threatened with suffocation in an unprecedented mass of water and mud. Property damages were approximately 100 billion dollars.

Hurricane Rita: The strongest hurricane since official measurements began. 119 deaths and damages around 20 billion dollars.

Hurricane Wilma: This was the strongest hurricane ever registered in the Atlantic. Maximal mean winds of 295 kilometers per hour and gusts of up to 340. Property damages amounted to approximately 29 billion dollars.

After Katrina and Rita, Wilma was the third category 5 hurricane. There had never before been 3 hurricanes of this category in one season.[54]

How does this accumulation of severe tropical storms develop?

- According to the region where they occur, tropical hurricanes bear different names, for example, typhoon in the Pacific, cyclone in the Indian Ocean, Willi-Willi in Australia and hurricane in the Caribbean. However, the mechanism by which they develop is the same. The basic condition for the development of a tropical hurricane is a water temperature of at least 27° C. This limits the regions where they can develop to tropical oceans between the northern and southern 15 degrees latitude.
The equator region itself remains free of hurricanes, because the Coriolis force needed for wind rotation is too low there. The Coriolis force is a natural phenomenon that can be explained by the earth's speed of rotation. When, for example, the winds from the northern Polar Region blow toward the equator, they are deflected toward

the right. But in the southern hemisphere it is just the opposite.

- The development of a hurricane begins when warm and very humid air rises from the ocean. Huge formations of cumulous clouds take shape and the energy stored by the evaporation of water is released in the upper atmosphere as condensation heat. This column of air becomes warmer than its surroundings and thus, lighter; and the atmospheric pressure over the ocean's surface strongly decreases. Like a vacuum cleaner, the developing hurricane sucks up more and more moist, warm air from its surroundings. It intensifies as it develops.

- We could describe tropical hurricanes as a huge atmospheric thermal engine. It transforms the energy stored in the heat of the tropical oceans and atmospheres into wind and waves. During the course of one day, an average hurricane releases 200 times as much energy as all the power plants in the world produce daily. A large hurricane can have a diameter of almost 1000 km and gusting winds of over 300 km per hour. The eye of the hurricane lies in the center of the storm with a diameter of 15 to 50 km, with an extremely low atmospheric pressure and almost no wind.

- An average hurricane dumps around 20 billion tons of rain per day. In some places, 2000 liters of water per square meter can fall in 1 or 2 days. This is about the amount of precipitation that falls in 3 to 4 years in central Europe. Hurricanes can produce waves up to 18 meters high that devastate entire coastal regions. A hurricane weakens as soon as it reaches land, because at that point, the supply of warm humid air is lacking. Global warming will most likely cause the intensity of hurricanes to increase. The oceanic regions over which a hurricane can form have grown more than 15% over the past 20 years. In addition, it is assumed that the increased warming of the oceans will extend the hurricane season by several weeks.

- The evaluation of meteorological data shows that a significant trend toward the intensification of low-pressure areas and deep depressions has been recorded in the northern region of the North Atlantic. It can be assumed from this that particularly during the winter months increased storm activity will develop over the North Atlantic.[55]

Tornadoes

- Tornadoes are extremely strong whirlwinds that are considerably smaller than tropical hurricanes, but can therefore reach higher wind speeds. In individual cases, wind speeds of over 700 km per hour have been measured. Tornadoes always develop in connection with strong thunderstorms when cold, dry air is pushed over warm, humid air. Tornadoes are typified by a pendulous, funnel-shaped cloud that marks its narrow path of greatest destruction. The air pressure in the tornado's center is extremely low, so that buildings over which the tornado moves may literally explode.

  The effects of a tornado are usually limited to a narrow band of somewhat less than 150 meters wide and 3 kilometers long. However, almost everything within this area is practically destroyed.

Above all, tornadoes occur mostly over the southern states of the US where the subtropical air from the Caribbean meets the cold continental air. Several tornadoes are often formed in the wake of a hurricane.[56]

Tsunami –
Flood Disaster in Southeast Asia

In the section on storms we read Christ's words through Gabriele from the year 1993:

Oh see, the storms of the times are not only forecast – they are blowing, raging, on all continents. But this is only the beginning. Whole continents are beginning to wobble, because the earth plates are rotating more and more, since the earth's magma is heating up ever more. And so, the entire earth is also heating up. You always think only of the atmosphere that is destroyed. But I say to you: The magma is heating up more and more and causing much to come into movement. The earth is heating up. The ice is melting. The floods are coming and the storms precede them ...

The Swiss reinsurance company Swiss Re spoke of an "abnormal accumulation of hurricanes" that caused 2004 to be the most expensive year for the insurance industry. And the storms really did precede the floods, because at the end of 2004 a tsunami set off a huge disaster.[57]

But here, too, God had given warning in time. Already in 1984 – 20 years ago – Christ told us the following:

51

Verily, verily, I say to you: The time is near when the waters will take many people away, when the planet earth will rebel and swallow up everything it can get hold of. And it will be that the waters will cleanse many parts of the earth ...

And in 1987 Brother Emanuel gave humankind a striking picture through Gabriele:

The mighty giant, the causal law – the giant bearing the many causes that people have created over the centuries and millennia, and much of which has not yet been atoned for – is going over the earth.

The mighty giant is stepping one time here and one time there. Wherever he puts his foot down, the causes begin and show the person what he, himself, has caused. He steps there: an earthquake, over there, another disaster; and there, a war begins. He steps there – atomic contamination, and he also steps in the oceans.

We human beings have set this "giant," so to speak, into motion. The flood disaster in Southeast Asia has shown us what effects it can have when he steps into the oceans.

- The disaster in Southeast Asia was triggered by an earthquake that occurred about 2:00 AM, Central European Time, on Dec. 26, 2004. It was the fourth strongest earthquake since 1900, with a magnitude of 9.0 on the Richter scale. The hypocenter of the quake was located 160 km west of Sumatra and 30 km deep, under the surface of the Indian Ocean. The earthquake was registered in various bordering countries, such as India, Bangladesh, Malaysia, Thailand, Myanmar, Singapore and the Maldives.

The earthquake was unusually large in its geographic extent. It occurred on a fault line where the Indo-Australian plate slid under the Burma plate. The Burma plate is part of the large Eurasian plate. It is estimated that approximately 1200 km of the Indo-Australian plate slid circa 15 meters under the Burma plate. This caused the Burma plate to rise between 10 and 30 meters, triggering shock waves in the Indian Ocean.

The earthquake unleashed gigantic quantities of energy, approximately as much as is needed to supply each of the 6 billion earth inhabitants with the energy to bring 5000 liters of water to boil. A large hurricane would need 70 days to release the same amount of energy.

The earthquake near Sumatra triggered a tsunami in the Indian Ocean. Tsunami is a word that comes from Japanese meaning "long harbor wave." They are usually triggered by earthquakes, but can also be caused by volcanic eruptions, nuclear explosions or the impact of a meteor in the ocean as well as underwater earth slides. The tsunami develops its destructive power only when it hits a coast. The waves that are only a meter high on the open seas turn into walls of water up to 30 meters, sometimes 100 meters, high when they hit the coast.

Tsunamis develop when large amounts of water become unbalanced, for example, through the movement up or down of the ocean floor. The waves spread out rapidly in circles from their origin, and the deeper the water, the higher the speed. In oceanic regions where the water is 4000 meters deep, the speed is about 700 km per hour. In the Pacific, it is known that where the water is 6000 meters deep, tsunamis can move at the speed of an airplane. As it approaches a coast, its speed is drastically reduced, while the wave reaches greatly increased heights.

Normally, tsunamis develop from a sequence of waves that hit the coast one after the other. Often the first crests are announced by a very deep ebb tide, followed by the wave. A tsunami wave can move 1 million tons of water; this means that the energy a tsunami brings with it when it hits the mainland is correspondingly large. The damage caused is enormous.

Much of the worst damage is caused less by the flooding itself, as by the suction that develops when the water withdraws. Entire houses, hotels and large buildings are washed away.

Tsunamis usually occur in the Pacific Ocean along the volcanic coasts, also known as the Ring of Fire, for example, the Philippines, Japan, Siberia, Alaska, USA, Guatemala, etc. This is why, already in 1948, a tsunami warning system was developed for the Pacific region that today encompasses 23 countries.[58]

- The last tsunami in the Indian Ocean occurred in 1883, triggered by the eruption of the volcano Krakatoa on an island near Java in Indonesia. The adjacent states had no early warning system, neither then nor in Dec. 2004. A system went into operation in Nov. 2008. The 2004 tsunami in the Indian Ocean was so powerful that at the western end of the Indian Ocean, more than 130 people are known to have died in countries along the East African coast in Somalia, Tanzania and Kenya, when waves swept 7000 km from the epicenter leaving a trail of smashed buildings and boats.[59]

- The earthquake on Dec. 26, 2004, occurred exactly 3 days after an earthquake measuring 8.1 on the Richter scale took place near the Auckland Islands, which lie between New Zealand and the Antarctic. Seismologists assume there could be a connection between the two quakes, since both epicenters lie on opposite sides of the Indo-Australian plate.

The earthquake near Sumatra occurred exactly (right down to the hour) one year after the great earthquake in Iran that destroyed the city of Bam. The earthquake caused a change in the earth's rotation, which, however, is classified as minor.[60]

There were no signs of seismological activity before the earthquake hit off the coast of Indonesia.

To get an impression of the devastation for people, we can read the following statistics in Wikipedia from August 2006: confirmed deaths, 184,164; estimated deaths, 230,210; missing persons, 45,752; displaced persons, 1.69 million persons.[61]

The extreme earthquake of Dec. 26, 2004 was followed by numerous aftershocks as well as two strong seaquakes in Southeast Asia (Mar. 28, 2005, 8.7 and Apr. 10, 2005, 6.8 on the Richter Scale). The seafloor before the west coast of Sumatra was shaken again on Sept. 12, 2007 by a severe seaquake, measuring 8.4 on the Richter Scale.

It was reported that this severe earthquake also caused a change in the earth's rotation. Although scientists have classified this change as minor, it can bring consequences. In 1986,

Christ explained the following interrelationships to us through Gabriele:

The so-called earth's axis, as you call it, will not only change, but it will also vary in its rotation – and thus the whole earth. Verily, I say to you: A force will form in the earth that will replace the earth's axis. But until then, some things will happen on the earth. The so-called earth's axis is changing and moving in a certain direction. Man would say that "it is bending." But this bend is not visible to humans. They sense it, because the seasons are changing; time is moving faster. The forces on and in the earth are indicating that great things are taking place from within to without, and it will happen! Through the strong deviation of the so-called earth's axis, the rotation, oceans are rising; earthquakes, volcanic eruptions and the like are following one after the other...

Anyone who remembers the first months of 2005 will no longer ask himself why the year started with unusually cold weather and an abnormal amount of snow in Europe despite a general climatic warming – the seasons are changing. Numerous earthquakes were also recorded during these months, above all in Turkey and Iran, but there was also the severe quake that took place again near Indonesia. At the same time, there were several volcanic eruptions in the greater Pacific area, one in Papua New Guinea, another in India on the Andaman Islands; Mt. Etna on Sicily is spitting fire and ashes again and at the same time, Mount St. Helens in the USA, and Popcatepetl and the Colima volcano in Mexico became active ... Only a few examples can be confirmed here, but perhaps you, dear reader, can identify such occurrences better now.

Forest Fires

God-Father said in 1997:
Mother Earth is shaking herself through storms, through forest fires and much more. She is calling: "You humans, what have you done to me?"

It is not only through storms that Mother Earth is shaking herself, but also through forest fires. And the divine world also spoke about this, but not for the first time in the year 1997, because as mentioned, Christ had warned people in 1991:
There is no going back! The floods are rising. The conflagrations are growing ever larger ...

Ever bigger conflagrations can be recognized by the following facts:

• With 808 million hectares, Russia has the largest forest area in the world. Between 2000 and 2005, an average of nearly 7 million hectares burned per year in Russia. 2003 was a year of extreme forest fires when circa 14.5 million hectares burned. According to the Ministry of Natural Resources, between March and mid-November of 2006, 25,200 forest fires were reported, which raged on an area of a total of 1.8 million hectares. (Source: Sukachev Institute of Forest)

• The USA has a total of 303 million hectares of forest area. A series of bad forest fires made the time period between 2000 and 2005 the worst since records have been kept. A total of 15.7 million hectares were consumed by flames.

In 2005 alone, it was circa 3.5 million hectares. (Source: FAO 2006)

The topic of "forest fires" also concerns the WWF, which released a report in 2007 entitled "Forests in Flame." The basis for the study reads: "Always when forest fires are too intense, in the wrong place, occurring at an unusual time or too often, it is a sign that the ecological system has been turned upside down through human intervention." In the following, you can read several of the dramatic facts presented in this report, facts that demonstrate how much man has already "turned the ecosystem upside down."

- Approximately 4% of all forest fires worldwide have natural causes, for example, a lightning strike. In all other cases, man is responsible for the fires – whether directly or indirectly, due to negligence or intentionally. Often the forest can no longer recuperate on its own, and not seldom, the burned areas and thus, the entire ecosystem, including the plants and animals that had lived there, is irretrievably lost.

- It is feared that after a certain percentage of forest area has been lost in the Amazon Basin – one of the largest rainforest regions on earth, in which forest fires are purposely set, for instance, to gain agricultural land for growing soybeans or for pasture for cattle – the regional climate will collapse. The resulting dryness would, combined with more forest fires, then destroy more rainforest. This would, in turn, have considerable effect on the global climate and worldwide diversity of species – a vicious circle. Presently, the percentage of forest lost or in extremely bad condition in the Amazon Basin is nearly 20%.

- In the Mediterranean region, the average area of forest fires has quadrupled since the 1960s. The causes lie mainly in negligence and deliberate arson, combined with extreme heat and dryness during summer months, as well as increasingly deteriorating forests, in which small fires can spread very rapidly. There are approximately 50,000 fires annually. Particularly hit are Spain, Portugal, Italy and Greece. In Spain, the number of forest fires has increased tenfold since the 1960s. In Portugal, a tenfold increase has taken place since 1980.

- In South and Southeast Asia, more than 40 million hectares were destroyed between 1990 and 2005. This represents an area nearly four times larger than the forestland in Germany. During the period from 1998 to 2002, 4.1% of the total forest area burned per year with a rising tendency.

- Through the greenhouse gases released during forest fires, they contribute considerably to global warming. As a result of global warming, the number and extent of forest fires rises, resulting in a feedback effect. Savanna and forest fires worldwide release 1.7 to 4.1 billion tons of carbon into atmosphere. In addition, an estimated 39 million tons of CH_4, 20.7 million tons of NO_x and 3.5 million tons of SO_2 are also added to this annually. Forest fires cause 40% of the worldwide emission of CO_2, 32% of CO, 10% of methane and over 86% of carbon-particulate emissions.[62]

Various studies assume that with the climate change, the number of days that have a high risk of forest fires will increase, the fire season will lengthen and the frequency of lightning strikes will rise, causing the frequency of forest fires to increase, as well as the size of the areas affected.

Drought: Famine and Lack of Water

The results of the climatic change are manifold. Rising temperatures cause more and more areas to dry up. In 1997, God, our Father, indicated that drought would become more and more prevalent. But the divine world had already made humankind aware of this.

Christ, 1990:
Humankind is holding up much externally – your politicians and your church leaders see to this. Everything that already exists is covered over, to the extent that people hardly hear about it. And yet, large parts of the earth are turning into steppes.

Famine is breaking out here and there. Many people are setting out to find food and to have shelter again. At the same time, the disasters are coming, not only nature disasters, but disasters to entire nations – because those who are starving, all those from whom everything external was taken, are becoming more and more aggressive.

We experienced how fast hunger and thirst drive people to aggression in April 2008, when the rapidly rising food prices led to unrest in numerous developing countries. The World Food Program (WFP) of the United Nations sounded an alarm, stating that between June 2007 and April 2008, the prices for food and fuel rose worldwide 55%. "As we are seeing in this 'new face of hunger,' sometimes people cannot afford food off the shelves, they need cash or voucher help for a targeted, short period of time..."[63]

But the face of hunger known to us has also increased dramatically in past years and will hit ever more people in the future.

- Already today, every third death among children worldwide is caused by malnourishment. 3.5 million children under the age of five die annually as a result of hunger. The World Hunger Report for 2007 stated that the number of people who do not have enough to eat is estimated at 854 million.[64]
  Particularly affected are African countries south of the Sahara and South East Asia. If the rising temperature cannot be slowed down, a further 600 million people are threatened with malnourishment, according to a report of the UN Development Programme (UNDP) released on November 27, 2007.[65]

- In February 2008, researchers at Stanford University in California presented a study with the alarming prognosis, that in approximately 20 years, the climate change will plunge whole regions into famine. According to the study, several of the poorest regions of the world must reckon with enormous crop shortfalls sooner than expected. In southern Africa, the yields of maize could drop nearly 30% during the next 20 years.[66]

- More than one billion people have no access to clean drinking water; 2.6 billion people have to live without sanitary facilities; that is about 40% of the world population. Worldwide 5000 children under the age of five die of diarrhea every day, because they and their parents do not know that dirty water makes you sick and can mean death, declared experts at the World Water Day in 2008. The main problem is that water is distributed unevenly. "Simply said, it is there, where no people live," said the French water expert Pierre Chevalier of the Paris Institute of Research for Development (IRD). "With the climate change, this will not get any better. It will promote evaporation and the melting of glaciers and lessen the amount of water available."
  At the same time, it was pointed out at World Water Day that for the production of one kilo of beefsteak, 15,000 liters of water are needed, while 1500 liters are needed for the production of one kilo of wheat. A human being needs two to five liters of drinking water per day.[67]

- According to the United Nations, circa 4 million people die each year of illnesses caused by polluted drinking water. Even all wars worldwide claim fewer victims annually.
  A shortage of water already prevails in 80 countries and according to the UN, the number of people affected will rise to more than 5 billion by 2030.
  Kofi Annan warned in March 2007, that up to 135 million people could flee their homelands due to drought – into areas where they would compete with local people for the available water. Some experts assume that lack of water could soon become the main cause of conflicts in Africa. [68]

- The NGO International Alert released a report in Nov. 2007 titled "A Climate of Conflict." We quote part of the introduction:

  There is a real risk that climate change will compound the propensity for violent conflict, which, in turn, will leave communities poorer, less resilient and less able to cope with the consequences of climate change. There are 46 countries – home to 2.7 billion people – in which the effects of climate change interacting with economic, social and political problems will create a high risk of violent conflict.

  There is a second group of 56 countries where the institutions of government will have great difficulty taking on the strain of climate change on top of all their other current challenges. In these countries, though the risk of armed conflict may not be so immediate, the interaction of climate change and other factors create a high risk of political instability, with potential violent conflict a distinct risk, in the longer term. These 56 countries are home to 1.2 billion people.

  The total equals more than half of the world population.[69]

- Water management in Asia is considered to be one of the most dangerous aspects of global warming. 400 million people are dependent on the Ganges River system and water levels are visibly falling. In addition, glaciers in the Himalayas are melting rapidly; between 1977 and 2000 the mean temperature there rose four times faster than the global mean temperature. Four of the largest rivers in Asia originate in the Himalayan region. The melting of the Himalayan glaciers will cause hundreds of millions of people to be first threatened by floods and then by lack of water.

Similar things are feared for South America. It is predicted that most of the glaciers in the Peruvian Andes will have disappeared by 2015. Two thirds of Peru's 27 million inhabitants live in coastal areas where natural springs cover only circa 1.8% of the water needed. So the cities as well as agriculture are dependent on the water from the mountains. [70]

- The climate change and direct interventions by man are causing the mountain chains to dry out worldwide. However, according to a study by the University of Bern, Switzerland, circa 7% of humankind is dependent on these drinking-water reservoirs. Considering the expected climatic changes and calculated regional population growth, the percentage of people dependent on water from the mountains could rise to 37% during coming decades.

But the climate change with its increasing warming is causing the mountains to lose their role as a "water tower." According to various studies presented at the general assembly of the European Geosciences Union (EGU) in Vienna, the runoff from the mountains is already decreasing. In Afghanistan, the number of its approximately 3500 glaciers is constantly shrinking because of decreasing precipitation.

Since 1985, the drinking water runoff in the areas that have been studied in the Alps has decreased circa 25%, and this, with constantly rising consumption on the plains. This could lead to a genuinely vicious circle, in which water consumption constantly rises, while resources decrease all because of rising temperatures. [71]

- The rise of ocean levels resulting from the climate change also threatens drinking-water reserves. Scientists at Ohio State University have found that saltwater penetrates much further underground than on the surface. According to the scientists, the consequences could be devastating. Nearly 40% of the world population lives in coastal areas, less than 60 km from the coast. These regions could lose more drinking water resources than previously thought.[72]

- While ocean levels are rising, more and more lakes are drying out. Here, we have the example of Lake Chad, which separates Nigeria, Chad, Cameroon and Niger. The lake has shrunk to barely 1/20 of its original size. While 40 years ago, the lake measured 38,850 square kilometers, a satellite picture from 2006 shows a surface area of 1,295 square kilometers. Global warming is to blame for this slow death of Lake Chad, as well as the extensive withdrawal of water. [73]

In the "Proceedings of the US Academy of Scientists," Canadian scientists warned that the climate change is causing thousands-of-years-old Artic lakes and ponds to dry out. John P. Smol of Queen's University in Kingston said in July 2007:
In the past researchers like us with our warning about global warming were often condemned as panic-mongers. Today we believe that we were much too optimistic. The speed and the extent with which the environment is changing are more dramatic than we imagined. [74]

- The Aral Sea, the northern part of which belongs to Kazakhstan and the southern part to Uzbekistan, was once the fourth largest inland sea in the world, fed by two mighty rivers. Since the beginning of the 1960s, the water of both rivers has been largely diverted, mainly to irrigate cotton fields. The result was that between 1960 and 1997, the surface of the sea shrank 44,3% to 29,630 square kilometers; the water volume sank 90% and the salt content quadrupled. In 2003, the surface area of the sea was only 18,240 square kilometers. Since 1966, circa 42,000 square kilometers of salt desert has developed. The highest children's mortality rate in the entire Soviet Union is recorded in the area surrounding the sea. People living near the Aral Sea are showing increased genetic damage, because the salty dust contains numerous poisons. The Aral Sea is considered a prime example of a man-made ecological disaster.[75]

- Since surface freshwater supplies are exhausted worldwide, groundwater reservoirs are being resorted to more and more often to supply drinking water. It is estimated that 1.5 billion people have meanwhile become dependent on groundwater. The most densely populated countries of China and India draw 50 to 100% of their water from groundwater. In China, in the area around Peking, the groundwater level has sunk in places from once 5 to 1000 meters. Groundwater is stored in so-called aquifers, underground layers of rock that store the groundwater and lead it on. The Ogallala aquifer in the USA is the most famous underground water reservoir worldwide. It supplies water to over 3.3 million hectares of farmland. This reservoir is being emptied 14 times faster than nature can refill it. In northern China, the underground reservoirs have already been pumped dry, causing the water supply to become ever more critical. The Great Lakes in North America contain 20% of the earth's freshwater supply. Their water levels have fallen to record lows during recent years.[76]

- In addition, chemical contamination of water is constantly increasing. Most of the waterways in the world are now highly poisoned. Lake Victoria in Africa is on the verge of biological collapse because millions of liters of untreated household and industrial wastewater are dumped into it. There are hardly any fish in the rivers of Senegal and Niger. In China 80% of the large rivers are so polluted that their complete stock of fish has died out. The Yellow River is so strongly polluted that its water can't even be used for irrigation.[77]

- The environmental report "Geo-4" published by the United Nations Environmental Program (UNEP) in October 2007 points out the following: In order to feed the increasing number of people, agriculture has been intensified. This is one of the greatest threats along with the climate change. Fertilizers contaminate drinking water and already today the irrigation of fields uses nearly two thirds of the fresh water available worldwide. Every tenth river no longer reaches the ocean. But the problem will get worse. During the coming 20 years, the developing countries, also because of eating more animal products, will need over 50% more water than today. Then, 1.8 billion people could be threatened with an absolute shortage of water.[78]

Consequences, which today are undeniable facts; however, Christ spoke of them already in 1990 when He said:

67

"Large parts of the earth are turning into steppes."
The following excerpt is from a message from Christ in 1994:
You talk about the earth's atmosphere. The atmosphere of the earth is a map of the world. Verily, I say to you that it looks dismal. Large areas are already dark. Its present condition points out what will be on the earth: incomparable chaos. Here and there the land dries and burns up; people suffer unspeakably under these influences. In the cities and in various places epidemics break out. Who asks about this already today? Who thinks about this already today? ... The deserts are expanding more and more. Storms contribute to this. They knock down everything that is no longer rooted ...
The earth is rebelling. In one place there is heat; in another, everything is burning; someplace else it is ice cold, everything freezing over ...

At that time, Christ spoke of the increasing desertification. In 2007 the UN said that increasing soil erosion resulting from the climate change and the excessive use of land for agriculture are a cause for famine, mass migration and war. According to estimates by the authors of a UN study on desertification, the advance of deserts is "the greatest ecological challenge of our time."

- Desertification threatens the existence of approximately two billion people, a third of the world population. About 41% of the arid areas worldwide are affected. Approximately 250 million people – primarily in Africa and Central Asia – are already feeling the effects of advancing deserts. A calculation by the experts makes the explosiveness of this situation clear: In ten years, up to 50 million people – the majority of them in Africa – will no longer be able to live where they formerly had been at home. For Yvo de Boer, the executive secretary of the United Nations Framework Convention on Climate Change, there is a close interrelationship between desertification and the global climate change.[79]

- The desertification of land in Africa is also a reason for the flow of refugees leaving the continent. According to the Algerian Minister for Planning and Environment, Cherif Rahmani, spreading deserts will cause 65 million Africans to seek refuge in industrial countries by 2025. [80]

- Twelve percent of the land surface of Europe is also threatened by advancing deserts. Large parts of the Mediterranean region, which was originally covered by thick oak forests, are acutely threatened by desertification. Today, only low copse woods are found around the Mediterranean. In Germany, it is also obvious that the ruthless use of land for industry is leaving behind sterile ground – a preliminary stage to desertification.[81]

- *Desertification is one of the greatest environmental and development problems of the 21st century. Some two billion people live in the world's drylands, whose biological productivity is under threat from the progressive deterioration of soils and other natural resources...* This is a quote from the introduction to the report on the international conference "Desertification and Security" held in Berlin in 2006. Desertification is the term used when soil becomes infertile and barren through intensive use. The problem is explosive. The basis of life for over one billion people is endangered because of the continuing loss of fertile soil. Desertification leads to famine and poverty, as well as social, economic and political tensions, which, in turn, can result in more conflicts, even more poverty and a further decline in soil quality.[82]

- Signs of desertification have meanwhile become visible in 70% of all drylands. In the year 2006, which was named "The International Year of Deserts and Desertification," 36 million square kilometers were affected, an area 3.5 times as large as Europe. In Africa, 40% of the total population lives in regions threatened by desertification, in Asia 39%, in South America 30%. These are particularly those developing countries that especially suffer under the destruction of land and resources. The fifty least developed countries are most strongly affected by desertification. In these countries, drylands cover approximately two-thirds of the land surface. [83]

- Worldwide, approximately two billion hectares of farm and pastureland have deteriorated to differing degrees. This is 15% of the land worldwide – it corresponds to an area the size of the United States and Mexico together. Nine million hectares thereof are irreparably destroyed and thus, permanently lost. Approximately one billion people live in the areas affected.
Worldwide, about five to seven million hectares of soil, which could be used for farming or grazing, are destroyed annually. This corresponds to an area the size of Ireland. Another 30 million square kilometers are acutely threatened by desertification. 25 billion tons of valuable topsoil are lost every year. This deterioration leads to an annual

loss of income, amounting to 42 billion dollars. Since the great drought of 1972-73, in the Sahel alone, circa 1.5 million hectares of agricultural land are lost every year.[84]

• The largest sand and gravel landscapes in the world, such as the Sahara in Africa or the Gobi Desert in Central Asia are moving ever further in the direction of civilization. More than 12 billion people are threatened. Up to 40% of the global land surface are already classified as drylands. All of southern Europe should prepare for an "Africanization" of the climate.[85]

• The situation in China is also dramatic. The living space of approximately 400 million people is threatened. Deserts are already covering 2.64 million square kilometers. This is one quarter of China's land surface.[86]

• A report released in Nov. 2007 by 17 Spanish climate experts states global warming is causing Spain to be threatened with "African conditions." They predict that one third of the Iberian Peninsula could become a desert by the end of the century. The climate change will cause desertification in large parts of Andalusia. The humidity in the air will decrease rapidly; temperatures will rise to over 50 degrees and by the end of the century rising ocean levels could cause several meters of beach to disappear. Climate researchers fear that approximately two thirds of Spain will be affected by this "Africanization." [87]

• According to the Commonwealth Scientific and Industrial Research Organization (CSIRO) in Australia, the water level in the Murray-Darling-River-System in southeastern

Australia, the most important farming region in the country, has fallen dramatically. In 2007, it was reported that after 12 years of drought, the annual amount of water flowing through the system has decreased from 11,400 to 4200 gigaliters.[88] According to a report in 2006, one Australian farmer commits suicide every four days.[89]

- North America is one of the regions with the most rapidly rising percentage of desertification. In the Great Plains, which comprise 1.3 million square kilometers in 10 states, the destruction of the natural vegetation cover through strong rains, agricultural methods not adapted to the area as well as cultivation and pasturage have led to extensive erosion. Already in the 1930s, the known problem of wind-caused erosion in the areas where wheat was grown led to the so-called "Dust Bowl." Devastating dust storms raged over the Great Plains. A result of plowing the prairie grasses so the land could be used for cultivation, years of drought led to fatal consequences. The deep roots of the prairie grasses had protected the upper soil layers from erosion, which now began on a massive scale. Harvests were destroyed by the dryness and the dust storms, resulting in the bankruptcy of more than one half a million farmers. [90]

Christ spoke about the fact that storms would contribute to desertification. It is shocking to read today what was meant by this:

- After evaluating the data in the "NASA Tropical Rainfall Measurement Mission," Israeli researchers concluded that sandstorms encourage desertification. Desert dust from sandstorms hinders the formation of clouds and rain. It thus promotes drought and the formation of deserts in far-distant regions. One would think that with their large grains of sand dust storms could bind a lot of water and lead to the formation of larger drops. But interestingly enough, the opposite is the case. According to the scientists' analysis, sandstorms are not the **result** of desertification and the formation of steppes, but are the **cause** of increasing dryness.

The advancing soil erosion caused by grazing herds of cattle and goats worsens the situation. As a result of the ever decreasing vegetation cover, sandstorms can carry more and more dust into the atmosphere. Scientists believe this is one of the important causes of the decades-long arid periods in the African Sahel Zone.[91]

- The number of sandstorms in Asia has increased fivefold since 1950. The South Korean capital of Seoul and cities in Japan are covered with yellow dust ever more frequently. This dust contains poisonous substances from Chinese industrial emissions.[92]

- It is estimated that in 2004 a total of two to three billion tons of sand were transported via sandstorms. One cause for increasing sandstorms is the use of all-terrain vehicles in the desert. They break up the thin, hardened crust on the desert surface, thus destroying the protection against erosion of the underlying sand.
  The introduction of cattle and sheep in the interior of Australia had the same effect. Their hooves destroyed the thin layer of vegetation.

Further causes are the increasing desertification, deforestation and climate change.[93]

Oceans

The disastrous way people treat the animal world, nature and the whole Mother Earth is leading to more and more disasters, the cause of which are we human beings. This can presently be seen in all the elemental forces. In the air, through the increasing frequency of storms, through the intensified solar radiation caused by the perforated atmosphere, and in the earth through drought. The element of water also brings man's causes into effect. This is visible not only through the rising oceans, through flood disasters and flooding, as we read in the chapter on climatic change, but also through the pollution of the oceans.

American scientists have ascertained the following:
The first-ever comprehensive map of our planet's marine environment shows that human activity has heavily affected 41 percent of the world's ocean-covered area, with no area left completely untouched. [94]

In 1984, Christ spoke to the people:
Look at the earth! What is happening to this shining planet? The heart of the earth, the oceans, are contaminated by atomic power and other pollutants. Rivers and lakes are polluted; atomic waste is put into the earth and into the oceans. What is happening? The oceans are heating up more and more; underground sources of water are contaminated; increased levels of mercury and lead

74

are radiated from the earth and the oceans are boiling. The polar caps are melting; the circulation of the earth is contaminated and is also being heated up. This is causing increased volcanic activity. Polar shifts are indicated, whereby the oceans will rise out of their basins and seek other basins. ...

And two years later, 1986, Brother Emanuel explained through Gabriele:

Atomic power pollutes not only the oceans, rivers, lakes and the earth. Atomic power heats up the oceans; the polar caps begin to melt. For your better understanding: The oceans are the stove; the earth is the burner on the stove. The oceans are heated up, the burner begins to glow.

While the effects are becoming clearly visible more and more with the melting of the polar caps and rising ocean levels, which we reported about in the chapter "Climate Change," most people know little about the cause – the contamination of the oceans through atomic power. Deliberately, hardly anything is ever talked or written about it. Here are some facts that make clear the extent of the atomic contamination:

• According to a report of the International Atomic Energy Association (IAEA), atomic waste lies stored on the ocean floors with an activity of 85 billion Bequerel. This is approximately as much as was contaminated by Cesium and Strontium during the Chernobyl disaster. In the Atlantic alone there are circa 250,000 containers lying at depths of 65 to 4750 meters. At the least, these are low-level to mid-level radioactive wastes, but, meanwhile, entire atomic reactors (from submarines) have also found their way there.

Sinking radioactive waste in the oceans was officially halted in 1993, but the reprocessing plants, for example, in Sellafield, England and La Hague, France continue to release discharges into the oceans as before.

Measurements taken by Greenpeace in the area of the wastewater pipes of the plants in La Hague (1997) and Sellafield (1998) showed shocking results. The ocean bottom around the pipes contains so much plutonium that, according to German law, the soil samples taken should be classified as atomic fuel. The contamination of ocean animals in the area such as crabs, mussels and fish is comparable to that after a large atomic accident.[95]

- Well-known, during the era of the Cold War, was the race between the superpowers for atomic weapons. Fifty years of weapon production in USA left behind dozens of millions of cubic meters of long-life nuclear waste. It has been calculated that a planned partial clean up will last 75 years and cost between 100 billion and 1 trillion US dollars – the costliest environmental clean-up program in history.

Even worse is the environmental pollution of the former Soviet Union. The region around the headwaters of the River Ob in Western Siberia is the most radioactive region on earth. 26 tons of plutonium have been accumulated there. After 1958, liquid wastes were deposited in Lake Karachai (South Ural mountains). In 1967, the lake dried out during a drought and dangerous dust, which was 3000 times as radioactive as the atomic bomb dropped on Hiroshima, spread over a region the size of Belgium. During the 1980s, anyone who stood for an hour on the shore of Lake Karachai received a fatal dose of radiation at 6 sievert/hour. The former head of the department for nuclear security in the USSR compared the situation to 100 Chernobyls.[96]

But it is not only through atomic power that the oceans are being polluted. In 1984, Christ spoke about other pollutions of the oceans in 1984. What consequences this will have can be read in the great divine work of revelation "This Is My Word"[97] (page 583), in which Christ made things clear to humankind in 1989:

Many animal and plant species – in the water, in the air and on the earth – are becoming extinct, because of the pollution of the rivers, lakes and oceans, as well as of the earth's atmosphere.

Until today, science has determined the following:

- The ocean conservation organization "Oceana" estimates that worldwide 675 tons of rubbish are thrown directly into the ocean every hour, one half of which is plastic. Circulating wind and water currents have caused a plastic carpet of approximately three million tons to form between California and Hawaii. It is half as large as Central Europe. More than 260 animal species have been verified to have fallen victim to the rubbish. Aside from fish, these include turtles, seabirds, seals and sea lions. Every year over a million seabirds and 100,000 sea mammals die a terrible death as a result of the trash that drifts on our oceans. Even if we human beings were to stop producing plastic tomorrow, the many millions of tons that have landed in the oceans up to now will drift with the currents around the world for thousands of years.[98]

- It is possible that the visible pollution in the ocean is not the greatest problem. The trash has an even more devastating effect as it slowly becomes invisible. Synthetic materials are gradually ground into smaller and smaller particles through solar radiation and the movement of the waves, until only a kind of powder is left. If this plastic powder is fine enough, it can even be swallowed by zooplankton and through this, make its way up the food chain, until it lands one day in our food. This scenario seems even more menacing when we consider the discovery of the geochemist Hideshige Takada from the Tokyo University of Agriculture and Technology. He found that plastic polymers act like a sponge for resilient poisons such as DDT and polychlorinated biphenyls. Takada's team found that non-water-soluble toxic chemicals can be found in plastic in levels as high as a million times their concentration in water.[99]

- Dead Zones in the Ocean: They can grow up to 70,000 square kilometers large, these "dead zones" in which all living beings die, because of the lack of oxygen. According to facts released by the United Nations Environmental Program, the number of these uninhabited regions in the world's oceans have meanwhile risen to 200. In 2004, it was 149.

  This increase has various reasons. A central role is played by the large amounts of nitrogen and phosphates from agriculture that land in the ocean via the rivers. Untreated waste water can also cause a lack of oxygen by promoting the growth of algae. Particularly in Africa, Asia and Latin America, 80% of the wastewater reaches the ocean untreated. [100]

"Science Daily" reported on Aug. 14, 2006, under the headline: *Dead Zone Causing Wave of Death off Oregon Coast*: *The most severe low-oxygen ocean conditions ever observed on the West Coast of the United States have turned parts of the seafloor off Oregon into a carpet of dead Dungeness crabs and rotting sea worms, a new survey shows. Virtually all of the fish appear to have fled the area. Scientists, who this week had been looking for signs of the end of this "dead zone," have instead found even more extreme drops in oxygen along the seafloor. This is by far the worst such event since the phenomenon was first identified in 2002, according to researchers at Oregon State University. Levels of dissolved oxygen are approaching zero in some locations. "We saw a crab graveyard and no fish the entire day," said Jane Lubchenco, the Valley Professor of Marine Biology at OSU. "Thousands and thousands of dead crabs and molts were littering the ocean floor, many sea stars were dead, and the fish have either left the area or have died and been washed away...* [101]

- The Three Gorges Dam in China:
  A huge 663-kilometer long dam is developing. In 2008, it is planned to have reached its final height of 175 meters. Houses, factories, streets, schools and cemeteries have sunk in the brown masses of water. The dam swallows industrial wastewater, hundreds of millions of cubic meters per year. It accumulates arsenic and strontium, sucks up the human wastes from millions of people and in addition, devours tons of chemical fertilizers that precipitation washes out of the fields. The dam is well on its way to becoming the planet's largest cesspool. [102]

Two million people have already been resettled and during the next ten years, 4 more million people will be resettled. This is four times as many as originally planned. The cause is the considerable deterioration of environmental conditions.[103]

- Worldwide 400 million tons of chemicals are produced annually and put into circulation by industry, agriculture and private persons. A part of this inevitably lands in the groundwater and in the rivers. A significant cause of water pollution is the antibiotics that are used in factory farming. In the European Union alone in 1999, 3900 tons of antibiotics were administered to fatten animals and 786 tons as performance-enhancers. Antibiotic residues reach the fields via manure slurry and seep into the groundwater.[104]

- During recent years increased hormonally active substances have been discovered in the water, so-called "endocrine disruptors." 70 substances have been determined that definitely have a disruptive effect on the sexual hormonal system and the thyroid gland. Additionally, there are circa 75 substances that are in all probability, hormonally active. Most of these 145 substances exhibit an estrogen-like activity. This can cause disturbances in the reproductive systems of animals and humans. The amphibian population in particular is decreasing worldwide at an alarming rate. A feminization of many fish species has been observed worldwide; this occurs when they come into contact with the wastewaters of sewage treatment plants.
The explosive nature of hormonally active substances consists of the fact that they add up in their effects. The concentration of an individual substance can lie under its thres-

hold of effect; but when several substances are combined, considerable hormonal effects are the result. [105]

- Sea snails from coastal waters worldwide demonstrate typical masculinization phenomena, which can be traced back to tributyltin compounds (TBT). TBT is a component of the anti-fouling paint used on ships; this paint prevents the growth of algae on ships' hulls. [106]

Thus far, some facts about the pollution of the waters and its consequences. One of the consequences, as we have read, is the extinction of species, but this holds true not only for aquatic animals, but also for many other species of plants and animals.

Extinction of Species

Let us bring to mind once more the words of Christ, which we can read in the divine work of revelation "This Is My Word" (pages 582-83):

Recognize that every animal senses and feels what a person intends to do with it. In the turn of time when I explain, correct and deepen the contents of that book [1989], brutality against the animal world and the plant world has reached unimaginable proportions. The animals and the plants suffer from man's capriciousness. Many people not only lack respect for their own life, but also for the entire creation ... Many animal and plant species – in the water, in the air and on earth – are becoming extinct, because of the pollution of the rivers, lakes and oceans, as well as of the earth's atmosphere – in the water, in the air and on the earth.

The brutality of people toward the animal and plant worlds truly has no limits. Just think of the suffering of the animals in factory farming, and during the transport and slaughtering of animals, and of the distress of the animals in woods and fields that have to live in constant fear of death at the hand of the hunters. The torments of the animals in experimental laboratories are indescribable and man has still more "traditions" with which he tortures animals. Thus, with his greed he partly contributes directly to the extinction of individual animal species. What significance this extinction of many animal and plant species has for us human beings becomes clear when we read what Christ explained to us about this in 1993:

O you people, are you aware that you cannot live without nature, without animals, plants and minerals? Many have not yet grasped this and have gone beyond the midway point; they have violated the earth and continue to violate it. In this way, they are even violating their own physical body.

Verily, verily, I say to you: Nature is the barometer for your life or death. If nature dies, then the human race will die. If nature blossoms, if it is healthy, then the human being is also healthy, and the human race will open up for the light. Many people open themselves for the darkness and violate the earth; they violate the animals, plants and minerals...

Using this barometer and basing ourselves on scientific fact, we can clearly see today where the human race stands.

In the online version of the British newspaper "The Telegraph," we could read the following on October 6, 2008:

The world is in the grip of an extinction crisis with thousands of species at risk of disappearing forever.

The survival of at least one in four land mammals is in doubt but it could be as high as one in three, according to the latest Red List of endangered species.

In the world's oceans and seas the situation is even worse with one in three marine mammals under threat.

Amphibians are also in severe trouble with 366 species added to the 2008 Red List. There are now 2,030 species – one in three – either threatened or extinct.

And a representative sample of reptiles shows that over one in five face a battle to survive.

Life on earth is disappearing fast with man inflicting most of the damage, according to the most comprehensive report of its kind drawn up by the International Union for Conservation of Nature (IUCN).

On land more species face oblivion because of loss of habitat, hunting and climate change while in the oceans pollution and the side effects of fishing are taking a huge toll.

An international research team made up of more than 1,700 experts in 130 countries compiled data for the world's 5,487 mammalian species including for the first time marine mammals. All the world's birds and amphibians were also assessed.

It revealed that at least 1,141 of the 5,487 mammals on earth are known to be threatened with extinction and at least half are in decline.

But because there is insufficient information on more than 800 species the figure could be much higher.

The areas of the world that have the richest biodiversity – such as south and southeast Asia – are among the most *threatened and where mammals face a bleak future. The report said 79 per cent of primates species in the region are threatened with extinction.*

The Red List reveals that 29 species have been flagged as Critically Endangered (possibly extinct) which means that in all probability – but not confirmed – the creature is extinct. It includes Cuba's Little Earth Hutia (Mesocapromys sanfelipensis), a small rodent, which has not been seen in almost 40 years.

There are 188 mammals in the Critically Endangered highest threat category which is only a step down from extinction. It includes the Iberian Lynx (Lynx pardinus), which is down to a population of just 84-143 adults.

Almost 450 mammals are listed as Endangered which is the next category down including the Tasmanian Devil (Sarcophilus harrisii), which moved from Least Concern to Endangered after the global population plummeted by more than 60 per cent in the last 10 years due to an infectious facial cancer.

Habitat loss and degradation caused by agriculture and deforestation affects 40 per cent of the world's mammals and is most extreme in Central and South America, West, East and Central Africa, Madagascar, and in South and Southeast Asia.

Over-harvesting is wiping out larger mammals, especially in Southeast Asia, but also in parts of Africa and South America.

Julia Marton-Lefèvre, IUCN director general, said: "Within our lifetime hundreds of species could be lost as a result of our own actions, a frightening sign of what is happening to the eco-systems where they live. We must now set clear targets for the future to reverse this trend and to ensure that our enduring legacy is not to wipe out many of our closest relatives."

Jan Schipper of Conservation International and lead author of a Red List article in Science, said: "The reality is that the number of threatened mammals could be as high as 36 per cent. This indicates that conservation action backed by research is a clear priority for the future, not only to improve the data so that we can evaluate threats to these poorly known species, but to investigate means to recover threatened species and populations."

But the IUCN report – the first since 1996 to include the conservation status and distribution of animals around the world – claims that species can be pulled back from the brink of extinction if conservation measures are taken. ...

Overall, the IUCN Red List now includes 44,838 species of flora and fauna of which 16,928 (38 per cent) are threatened with extinction.

Of these, 3,246 are in the highest category of threat, Critically Endangered, 4,770 are Endangered and 8,912 are Vulnerable to extinction.[107]

- The extinction of species is a normal part of evolution, but human influence is causing the tempo to rise exponentially. It is estimated that for 200 million years on the average one species became extinct per year. Since 1985, the rate is one species per hour and since 2000 one species per 30 minutes! The World Wildlife Fund (WWF) estimates the disappearance of 25,000 plant and animal species each year. [108]

- According to a recent study published in the magazine "Science" on Sept. 10, 2004, the extinction of plants and animals sets a chain reaction into motion. This can mean, for instance, that the disappearance of a single species, such as an South American ant, can threaten the basis of existence for up to 100 kinds of birds, beetles and mites. Scientists warn that the number of endangered species up until now doesn't reflect the whole picture.[109]

- Above all, logging rainforests leads to the extinction of many animal and plant species, for the tropical rainforests are centers of the global diversity of species. They cover only 6% of the earth's land surface, but shelter more than half of all known species of organisms. In the Amazon rainforest more plant and animal species are found on an area of 10 square kilometers than in all of Europe.

According to the Food and Agricultural Organization of the United Nations (FAO), the deforestation rate of all tropical rainforests has been approximately 1% per year since the 1980s. Every year an area equal to half the size of Florida disappears. The rainforests of the West Indian islands, the Brazilian Atlantic coast, Madagascar and the Philippines have already shrunk to less than 10% of their original size.[110]

- The earth has lost approximately 3% of its green mantle in 15 years, a forest area of more than three times the size of Germany. This figure was taken from the forest report of the Food and Agriculture Organization of the United Nations (FAO) in 2007. The worst deforestation is taking place in Africa, Latin America and the Caribbean.[111]

- In Brazil alone, the Amazon rainforest covered circa 4.1 million square kilometers. Meanwhile, it has shrunk to 3.4 million square kilometers. Thus, 17% of this unique habitat is irretrievably lost. From 2002 to 2006, an average of nearly 2.15 million hectares were destroyed annually – this corresponds to 4.1 hectares, or almost 6 football fields, per minute![112]

  In Brazil, the forests suffer especially from raising animals for meat, and this, in two ways. Huge pastures are created, above all, for cattle. However, the large landowners also need ever more new fields for growing enormous amounts of soybeans. This energy-rich feed is used all over the world in factory farming. Thus, the greed for cheap meat in the rich countries is eating up the South American rainforests.

- The continuing deforestation of the largest tropical forest threatens not only plant diversity. Researchers' computer simulations predict that the destruction of the rainforest could trigger a great drought. Chain reactions in the atmosphere would shift the polar jet stream and thus, also the precipitation it brings with it. Jet streams are fast-flowing, relatively narrow air currents found in the upper layers of the atmosphere, with high vertical and horizontal wind speeds. The lack of precipitation could even lead fertile rainforests to turn into dry savannas.

  However, the plant world not only has a great influence on precipitation, but also on the CO_2 balance of the land. According to a WWF report, the trees in the Amazon store 90 to 140 tons of carbon dioxide. This corresponds to the amount released by human activities in 9 to 14 years. The deforestation of the forests – whether by clear cutting or decay – already now releases up to 400 million tons of carbon dioxide into the atmosphere; this is 80% of the greenhouse gases produced in Brazil.[113]

- In Indonesia 400 square kilometers of virgin forest are destroyed annually, for the German market of tropical wood alone. Wood products stemming from illegal sources worth 1.2 billion euros are imported into the European Union every year. According to information from the World Wildlife Fund (WWF), approximately 80% of the tropical wood products on the German market are from illegal sources.[114]

Likewise, according to information from the WWF, we can assume that until the year 2020 approximately 22 million hectares of virgin forest and savannah in South America will fall victim to increasing soybean farming. The worldwide demand for soy products is forecast to rise 60%, mainly from China and Europe, where soybeans, genetically modified for the most part, are used on a large scale to fatten animals on factory farms. In 2003, the EU alone imported 30 million tons of soy meal as animal feed.[115]

- British researchers have looked back at the history of life over a period of 520 million years and have found an ominous correlation: Each of the five known great periods of mass mortality in the history of the earth was connected to a rise in temperature. The researchers warn that if people continue to heat up the earth with greenhouse emissions, this threatens the diversity of species and further mass mortality in the near future cannot be ruled out. This was published in an article in the "Proceedings of the Royal Society B."[116]

If scientists are already talking of mass mortality and we remember the statement of the Spirit of the Christ of God from the year 1993, that nature is the barometer for our living or dying, what makes us so sure that the "species man" will survive this dying?

Extinction of Species – What Will Become of the Species Man?

Scientists are presently talking about the extinction of plants and animals over and over again and are already developing their own ideas to provide for an emergency. In 2008, a project on Spitsbergen made large headlines. A "modern remake of Noah's Arc," as it was described by politicians, was opened on the Artic island, in which 4.5 million seed samples from agricultural plants are to be stored in a seed vault. This refrigerator for crop plants, "a frozen Garden of Eden," as the President of the European Commission, José Manuel Barroso, described it, was built 120 meters deep into the earth, 130 meters above the current ocean level, so that even in case a large part of the ice cover melts, no water can penetrate it. It was said that the seeds, protected by high and thick cement walls, would also survive an atomic war or other global disasters.[117]

What causes scientists and politicians to undertake such a cost-intensive project? Do they perhaps know more than they admit to humankind? Have they already given up on the earth? Questions to which we will receive no answers from science or politics, but which give us an inkling of where the world stands today.

Several scientific projects to counter the extinction of animal species – officially to preserve genetic information – such as the "Frozen Arc" of the Natural History Museum in London or the "Frozen Zoo" in the USA, have been started. The goal of these projects is to collect the genetic material, that is, tissue and DNS samples from species threatened with extinction, and to preserve them frozen for posterity. Ostensibly, these global gene databanks are to be a resource of knowledge, which should give information about the evolution of the species and their changes over the course of the history of evolution. But not a few scientists hope to one day produce genetic clones from the frozen DNS material, in order to let extinct animals "resurrect" again. But in which habitat should the animals then be resettled? In the habitat that was so destroyed by man that the species died out? [118]

Aside from storing plant seeds and deep-freezing animal genes, scientists of the European Space Agency (ESA) have given thought to a databank on the moon, in order to make access to presently existing knowledge possible for survivors of a worldwide disaster. The scientists would like to have the first databank placed on the moon by 2020; the goal is that it has a lifespan of 30 years. The open question is only how survivors should receive this information after a disaster on earth. Here, too, we can only pose the question: What moves scientists to reflect on such projects. What kinds of global disasters are they thinking of? [119]

However, it is more than questionable whether these measures can save us from what Christ revealed in 1993:

Nature is the barometer for your life or death. If nature dies, then the human race will die.

Interesting scientific facts about this were published in a study conducted at Cornell University in Ithaca, New York:

About 40 percent of deaths worldwide are caused by water, air and soil pollution, concludes a Cornell researcher. Such environmental degradation, coupled with the growth in world population, are major causes behind the rapid increase in human diseases, which the World Health Organization has recently reported. Both factors contribute to the malnourishment and disease suscepti-bility of 3.7 billion people, he says.

David Pimentel, Cornell professor of ecology and agri-cultural sciences, and a team of Cornell graduate stu-dents examined data from more than 120 published papers on the effects of population growth, malnutrition and various kinds of environmental degradation on human diseases. ...

"We have serious environmental resource problems of water, land and energy, and these are now coming to bear on food production, malnutrition and the incidence of diseases," said Pimentel.

Of the world population of about 6.5 billion, 57 percent is malnourished, compared with 20 percent of a world population of 2.5 billion in 1950, said Pimentel. Malnu-trition is not only the direct cause of 6 million children's deaths each year but also makes millions of people much more susceptible to such killers as acute respiratory in-fections, malaria and a host of other life-threatening diseases, according to the research.

Among the study's other main points:

• Nearly half the world's people are crowded into urban areas, often without adequate sanitation, and are exposed to the epidemics of such diseases as measles and flu.

• With 1.2 billion people lacking clean water, waterborne infections account for 80 percent of all infectious diseases. Increased water pollution creates breeding grounds for malaria-carrying mosquitoes, killing 1.2 million to 2.7 million people a year, and air pollution kills about 3 million people a year. Unsanitary living conditions account for more than 5 million deaths each year, of which more than half are children.

• Air pollution from smoke and various chemicals kills 3 million people a year. In the United States alone about 3 million tons of toxic chemicals are released into the environment – contributing to cancer, birth defects, immune system defects and many other serious health problems.

• Soil is contaminated by many chemicals and pathogens, which are passed on to humans through direct contact or via food and water. Increased soil erosion worldwide not only results in more soil being blown but in spreading disease microbes and various toxins.[120]

The numbers in this study are shocking; according to them, four out of ten people die as a result of environmental pollution today. A year before, (2006) WHO estimated the percentage of environmental deaths at 23%. What will the future bring?

We received a clear indication of this already in 1998 from the spiritual world through Brother Emanuel, who spoke to us through Gabriele:

Now think along with me. First the nature kingdoms will die, including the animals, because allegedly they were there first, before human beings. Countless plant and animal species are dying out. Humankind cannot live without nature. And so, the death will come with nature, you would say: afterward. First nature, the animals, and then the human beings.

I say to you: This earth will turn into steppes more and more. The waters will seek new streams and new basins. The volcanic activity must increase even more, because the innermost part of the earth is fertile. The lava will cover up whatever refuse is there, which man created in order to torment the earth, to maltreat it, perhaps even wanting to kill it – but that is impossible.

And so, many of the "great ones" reach for the stars and think there must be life somewhere in the cosmos, so as to be able to continue to live there. Life is everywhere – but not for these people.

Oh see: So this human race will also die out. But you could always come again ..."

The dying of the human race will be introduced through the natural disasters that Brother Emanuel spoke of already in 1986. But he spoke not only of natural disasters, but also revealed the following words through Gabriele:

But the disaster also continues among the people: The climate is changing; the people are being heated up; the nervous system becomes tense.

All that a person has stored in his consciousness, subconscious and in his soul garments is coming into effect. What is happening on this earth? Murder, hostility, rivalries, civil wars ...

The divine world gave warning of impending civil wars already in 1986. At the world climate conference on Bali in December 2007, the leading German climate expert, Hans Joachim Schellnhuber, the director of the Potsdam Institute for Climate Impact Research, also warned about this and said that the continued global warming could even lead to "global civil war."[121]

Whether these disasters can still be averted is questionable. However, the warnings from the divine world came in time, because 17 years earlier, Christ spoke the following admonishing words through Gabriele:

Large parts of the earth are turning into steppes. Famine is breaking out here and there. Many people are setting out to find food and to have shelter again. At the same time, the disasters are coming, not only natural disasters, but disasters to entire nations – because those who are starving, all those from whom everything external was taken, are becoming more and more aggressive. They seize all possible objects that they can then make into weapons against their neighbor, in order to plunder, to get, to procure what they can still obtain for their body.

And in 1992, Christ gave us a picture that we can understand more and more today:

The earth can be compared to a scale. In one of the scale pans is the South, in the other scale pan is the North. The scale pan of the North is tilted; the scale pan of the South is pouring over the North. Happy the one who recognizes this sign and saves himself.

Meanwhile, the politicians of the European Union also see these dangers and since March 2008 classify the global climate change and its effects as a political security risk and a threat to Europe.

- According to a statement by the European Union foreign affairs chief, the climate change has a "threat multiplier" effect, because it increases already existing tensions and instability. Risk factors include conflicts for water, food and energy resources, threatening floods in huge coastal cities, the disappearance of whole stretches of land and islands and the resulting border conflicts and waves of refugees in developing countries.

  Particularly threatened regions are the African continent, the Middle East, South Asia, Central Asia, Latin America and the Arctic. As a probable consequence of increased tensions and instability caused by the climate change "threat multiplier," the EU document describes huge streams of refugees pouring into the EU.[122]

- In 2008, Karsten Smid, the climate expert of Greenpeace, spoke of 20 million people who are presently fleeing from the consequences of the climate change – this is more than 50% of all refugees worldwide. In 2007 Greenpeace published a study on the situation of climate refugees, which arrived at the conclusion that during the next 30 years, 200 million people will leave their homelands, because their living conditions will grow ever worse as a result of the climate change.[123]

And at Christmastime 1998, God, our heavenly Father, warned us in a divine message from the All through His prophetess and messenger, Gabriele:

95

What is standing before the door of the world? Chaos. Earth disasters. Globally spoken: the deluge, which will afflict the sinners. Continents will disappear; parts of continents will fall victim to the waters. And many a country will slide into the abyss. Your mountains will pass away, because the valleys will fill with water. Where, where then, is your highly lauded heritage, which you inherited from your fathers, money and property, goods, lands, possessions, etc., etc.? Under the lava? Under the waters? In order to retrieve all of it, you must become divers – or laborers, so as to remove the rocks. Or will you build your so-called poorhouses on them?

Verily, I say to you: Little land will remain fertile. The people do not cherish the great unity, the brotherliness; they live as individuals and will thus fall victim to the floods of the world.

- In November 2007, the London research group International Alert presented its report entitled "A Climate of Conflict." We can read the following in it:
There are 46 countries – home to 2.7 billion people – in which the effects of climate change interacting with economic, social and political problems will create a high risk of violent conflict.
There is a second group of 56 countries where the institutions of government will have great difficulty taking the strain of climate change on top of all their other current challenges. In these countries, though the risk of armed conflict may not be so immediate, the interaction of climate change and other factors creates a high risk of political instability, with potential violent conflict a distinct risk in

the longer term. These 56 countries are home to 1.2 billion people.[124]

In the divine message previously quoted, our Father also said that the mountains will pass away and the valleys will fill with water. New scientific knowledge reveals the following:

- The temperatures in the Alps are rising twice as fast as the global average. Permafrost, which for thousands of years has sealed whole mountain ranges like cement, is threatening to melt. This could cause whole mountainsides to begin to slide. The permafrost, also called eternal ice, glues together crevices and cracks. When the permafrost melts, the rock will crumble and disintegrate and then fall down.[125]

- The probability of large rockslides in the Alps is increasing with continued warming and ice melt. Since the mid-1980s, there have been 7 rockslides with over a million cubic meters of stone registered. It is quite certain that permafrost was involved in four of the slides.[126]

- Between 500,000 and 700,000 cubic meters of rock broke off from the east flank of the Eiger in the Swiss Alps in July 2006. This amount of material corresponds in volume to approximately one half of that of the Empire State Building in New York. Geologists are of the opinion that the retreat of the Grindelwald glacier contributed to the rockslide.
  The diminishing weight of the ice causes the rock to expand and tensions can be discharged. Furthermore, water can penetrate into the rock.[127]

- In 2002, the United Nations Environmental Program (UNEP) published a study that warned of catastrophic floods caused by melting glaciers in the Himalayan region. With their high water level, 44 glacial lakes represent a real threat to the valleys and large drainage areas. Through the rapid rise of the glacial lakes, which were dammed up by ice, debris and coarse gravel, floods could be triggered by dam breaks. Such dangerous potential also exists in the Andes.[128] Researchers from the Centre for Integrated Mountain Development (ICIMOD) in Nepal concluded in 2006 that every 200 to 300 years there were flash floods of catastrophic potential, but now they predict their occurrence every two to three years. The reason for this is the climate change with its global warming. This is causing hundreds of glaciers to melt at an ever increasing tempo and thus retreat. For example, the tongue of the Kongma Tikpe glacier in Nepal: It retreated 60 centimeters per year (1976 to 1978), then about 2.5 meters per year (1978 to 1989) and the most recent measurement shows it was reaching ten meters annually (1989 to 2004).[129]

- Because of the draining glacier lakes, there is also danger of flash floods in the Alps. For instance, there is an area in Bernese Oberland at the foot of the Trift glacier. Between 2000 and 2005, the glacier shrank over 500 meters – approximately 7% of its present length of 7.1 kilometers. Since 1980, the glacier has been losing about nine million cubic meters of ice annually. This rapid melting has consequences. Since 1998, a lake has formed around the glacier's tongue in the shape of a half circle – a typical symptom of the climate change as can be seen with many alpine glaciers. With the retreat of the Trift glacier's tongue, not only the lake grows; at the same time the ice masses in the lower part of the glacier will be lacking their supporting base in the near future. A hanging glacier will form on the steep side. Up to six million cubic meters of ice will then hang over the lake like a Damocles sword. The danger of an ice plunge is growing. It could plunge into the lake and trigger a kind of tidal wave, with devastating consequences for those living in the valley.[130]

Volcanoes and Earthquakes

Many of the earth upheavals and disasters presented so far are already visible and are developing ever more swiftly and drastically. Other disasters with grave consequences could suddenly hit humankind; these include volcanic eruptions and earthquakes, for instance. In the messages from the All quoted previously, the divine world warned us of this over and over again. Let us bring to mind the words of Christ through Gabriele in February 1984:

Look at the earth! What is happening to this shining planet? The heart of the earth, the oceans, are contaminated by atomic power and other pollutants. Rivers and lakes are polluted; atomic waste is put into the earth and into the oceans. What is happening? The oceans are heating up more and more; the underground sources of water are contaminated; increased levels of mercury and lead are radiated from the earth and the oceans are boiling. The polar caps are melting; the circulation of the earth is contaminated and is also being heated up. This is causing increased volcanic activity. Polar shifts are indicated, whereby the oceans will rise out of their basins and seek other basins. The mainland that is under water is rising and the present mainland will be largely flooded. All at once, the volcanoes will roar, there will be earthquakes and people will fight each other.

Brother Emanuel explained something similar in August 1986, in a divine message that was previously cited:

The oceans are the stove; the earth is the burner on the stove. The oceans are being heated up, and the burner begins to glow. All these negative vibrations have their effect on souls and human beings; earthquakes, volcanic eruptions and the like are the so-called natural disasters.

And as early as a month later, in September 1986, Christ spoke through Gabriele:

The forces on and in the earth are indicating that great things are happening from within to without; and it will happen! Through the strong deviation of the so-called earth's axis, the rotation, the oceans are rising; earthquakes, volcanic eruptions and the like are coming one after the other.

And several months before, in June 1986, Christ said:

Death comes along and will sweep many away. Fear will increase; civil wars and wars will develop. Volcanoes will erupt, to cleanse the earth. Lava will flow over many stretches of land and cover up what is unlawful, yes, damaging to the earth, to man and the atmosphere.
And the forces of infinity will work the lava, so that it makes the earth fertile again. Here and there the oceans will seek other basins and in this way, the earth will

cleanse itself. Through inner movements, through earthquakes, it will be torn apart, and what is not lawful will sink into the crevices.

The divine world continued to give warning and Brother Emanuel spoke through Gabriele in October 1989, in a message quoted earlier:

Recognize that through man's causes the earth has become a fiery oven. Layers of the atmosphere are dissolving – the world is like a pressure cooker that is standing on the earth; it is boiling. What happens? The continental plates are moving faster and faster – they are traveling, wandering. This triggers more disasters: earthquakes, volcanic eruptions and much more.

In a mighty message from the Creator in November 1997, God-Father raised His voice through Gabriele as a plaintiff for the Mother Earth, saying:

And at all times, the people do not listen to the call of the tormented earth, to say nothing of the word of God through the prophets, through spiritually enlightened men and women, through fighters for the kingdom of the inner being. And so, the mouth of the earth, of Mother Earth, is opening up. It is the volcanoes. And the Mother Earth calls: "I can no longer carry you now! – peace, peace, peace," she calls. And the lava flows out of her mouth and covers great parts of the earth.

There are numerous messages from the All, in which the divine world pointed to volcanic eruptions and earthquakes. The "International Strategy for Disaster Reduction" (ISDR) is already recording a slight increase in geological disasters, that is, earthquakes, tsunamis and volcanic eruptions. But even when there is no specific information from the side of science as to when a volcano will erupt or an earthquake will take place, there are several shocking indications:[131]

- Approximately 80% of the world population lives in agglomerations along the edges of the earth's continents. Most raw materials are found there as well as access to the ocean, that is important both economically and militarily. However, the edges of continents often mean that the large cities are in earthquake and volcanic zones, in addition to being close to the ocean, which can always cause storms and floods.

- Dozens of large cities lie in areas where earthquakes are likely to happen. This information was made known in 2006 with the publication of the "World Stress Map." Particularly endangered is Tokyo with its 30 million inhabitants, "the city waiting for its death," as Bill McGuire, a hazards researcher at University College London, drastically formulated. And many other megacities lie in earthquake zones. The danger is growing, because according to the United Nations most cities double their population within 15 years. In the year 2016, there will be 25 cities with more than 10 million inhabitants located in earthquake regions. The geologist Roger Bilham from the University of Boulder in Colorado, USA, prognosticated that soon there will be 1 million people who die from earthquakes per year. During this century, there will be such terrible earthquake disasters as never before.[132]

- According to a 2008 study conducted by the US Geological Survey and the Southern California Earthquake

Center, it is nearly 100% certain that California will be hit by a severe earthquake within the next 30 years. The probability of a severe earthquake measuring 6.7 by the year 2038 is 99.7%. An even more severe quake of a magnitude of 7.5 or more has a 46% probability, according to the scientists.[133]

- Melting ice sheets lead not only to the rising and bulging of the surface of the earth as a result of less weight, but also to strong changes in the tension fields in the earth's crust. A study by the Institute of Geology and Paleontology at the Westphalia Wilhelm's University in Münster, Germany, confirms that climate fluctuations can decidedly influence the seismicity of the earth's crust, and brings up the question of whether the present melting of inland ice – for example in Greenland – could trigger earthquakes in the future.[134]

- According to the Munich Reinsurance Company, there are about 550 volcanoes in the world that are classified as active. Today, just as over 25 years ago, it is still true to say that – with the exception of extremely rare major meteorite impacts – there are no other natural events that can devastate such wide areas with comparable intensity and suddenness as volcanic eruptions. Their direct effects: lava, mud and pyroclastic flows, glowing clouds, ash eruptions, and ash deposits. The indirect effects: climate change. The losses: aside from direct losses, disruption of air transport and shipping and crop failures.[135]

- A warmer world could be a more explosive one. Global warming is having a much more profound effect than just

103

melting ice caps – it is melting the magma, too. Vatnajökull is the largest ice cap in Iceland, and it is disappearing at a rate of 5 cubic kilometers per year. Carolina Pagli of the University of Leeds, UK, and Freysteinn Sigmundsson of the University of Iceland have calculated the effects of this melting on the crust and magma underneath. They say that, as the ice disappears, it relieves the pressure exerted on the rocks deep under the ice sheet, increasing the rate at which it melts into magma. An average of 1.4 cubic kilometers has been produced every century since 1890, a 10% increase on the background rate.

In Iceland there are several active volcanoes under the ice. The last big eruption was in 1996 at Gjàlp, and before then in 1938 – a gap of 58 years. But Pagli and Sigmundsson say that the extra magma produced as the ice cap melts could supply enough magma for similar eruptions to take place every 30 years on the average. Predicting the eruptions precisely will be tricky, though, as the rate of magma migration to the surface is unknown.

The situation in Iceland does not necessarily mean magma will be melting faster around the world. Vatnajökull sits atop a boundary between plates in the earth's crust, and it is this configuration that is allowing the release in pressure to have such a great effect deep in the mantle.

But the thinning ice has another effect on volcanoes that will be more widespread. As the amount of weight on the crust changes, geological stresses inside the crust will also change, increasing the likelihood of eruptions. "Under the ice's weight, the crust bends and as you melt the ice the crust will bounce up again," explains Bill McGuire of University College London in the UK, who was not involved in the study.

McGuire thinks the Vatnajökull study is based on "perfectly reasonable" physics. However, he says that climate change presents an even more explosive threat. "It's not just unloading the crust that triggers volcanic activity but loading as well." He and his team are looking into the effects that rising sea levels – also a consequence of melting ice caps – will have on volcanoes. "We are going to see a massive increase in volcanic activity globally," he told "New Scientist." "If we look back at previous warm periods, that is what happened." [136]

- Circa 500 million people live near volcanoes. Volcanic eruptions particularly threaten the following metropolises: Mexico City, Manila, Jakarta, Naples and Seattle. Also endangered are Hawaii, Tenerife and Crete. There is also a high risk in Japan. Besides Tokyo, the millions-cities such as Nagoya, Kyoto and Yokohama are threatened. The area around Mt. Fuji would also be hit hard – 20 million people spend their vacations there every year. [137]

- Commissioned by the British government, the Geological Society of London put together an expert report – with troubling results.
  In Europe alone, two gigantic volcanoes are waiting for their next eruption. The British geologists think they have identified two super volcanoes: under the Phlegraean Fields near Naples and in the eastern Mediterranean near the island of Kos.
  The experts also assume the natural danger under New Zealand, Kamchatka, the Philippines, the Andes, Central America, Indonesia and Japan. Super volcanoes have a

huge magma chamber with an expansion of thousands of square kilometers, which typically extend into depths of 5 to 20 kilometers.[138]

- The volcanoes in the Eifel (a plateau in western Germany, northwest of the Moselle and northeast of Luxemburg) are not extinguished by far; they are merely resting. Every year the Eifel rises a millimeter. The experts agree that eruptions will take place in the Eifel again. According to the volcanologist Hans-Ulrich Schmincke of the Leibniz Institute for Oceanography in Kiel, Germany, the Eifel is presumably at the beginning of a new phase of activity. He has researched the volcanoes in the Eifel for years. Worldwide, volcanoes follow analogue cycles. In an expert report for the German government in 2001, the geophysicist Gerhard Jentzsch from the University of Jens wrote that if things follow the same pattern in the Eifel, numerous eruptions are to be expected.[139]

- An especially disastrous volcanic eruption could take place in Yellowstone National Park. There, a magma reservoir is expanding over an area double the size of Luxemburg. The magma is gradually penetrating upward and melting the earth's crust; an eruption appears possible. A disaster occurs there about every 700,000 years; the last large eruption was 640,000 years ago. Satellite observations show that the park is bulging like a bubble – several millimeters a year. The pressure of the underground magma chamber is becoming ever more noticeable, said geologist Robert Smith of the University of Utah in Salt Lake City. In November 2007, scientists of the University of Utah published suspected record-breaking changes in the magazine "Science." Within 30 months, the surface of the crater rose a total of 18 centimeters, more than ever before since taking measurements began in 1923.

An eruption of the volcano would totally devastate western USA. In the region surrounding the volcano, 800°C hot avalanches of lava, ashes and stone would destroy all life on an area the size of Thuringa, Germany. In Los Angeles, ca. 1300 km away, rain would fall that would cover the region with a 30 cm thick layer of ashes. The scientists associated with Steve Sparks and Stephen Self of the British Geological Society predict that agriculture would be impossible in many places. A layer of only one centimeter would destroy the yield of a field. The climate would be gravely changed. Billions of tons of sulfur dioxide would enter the atmosphere and combine with water to produce sulfuric acid. Clouds consisting of acid drops would surround the globe like a sunshade. For years the temperatures would be an average of 4°C lower. On the northern hemisphere it is possible that it would cool up to 10°C, as stated in an report based on a computer simulation conducted by the renowned Hadley Center.

When will this horror scenario take place? Based on the frequency of eruptions in the past, British researchers have estimated the risk: The probability of an eruption taking place during this century is 1 to 6.[140]

How the apocalypse of a volcanic eruption announces itself is not yet known by scientists. Usually, earthquakes precede an eruption; escaping gases change; the temperature of the soil rises; the ground bulges. The super volcanoes of the Phlegraean Fields and Yellowstone are already being monitored for these signs. Whether this is of any use is questionable.

Because it is possible that the sleeping giants will awaken without any advance notice and explode with a sudden bang.

The Polar Shift

A few years ago, this topic earned the Original Christians the reputation of being end-time apostles or end-time fanatics from the church "department for disinformation and slander" and the media subservient to this department. Today many media reports refer to an impending polar shift. For example, in the February 2006 issue of the German magazine about science and technology "PM," the question: *When will the poles shift?* was answered as follows: *They are already doing it, and at a relatively fast pace.* The article closed with the statement: *The last polar shift took place 750,000 years ago, making the next one long overdue.* This topic is often taken up on television. In June 2004, on ZDF (a German public television station) the following was said during the course of the Evening News: *The magnetic poles of our earth – north and south – are well on their way to exchanging positions, thus finally putting the world literally on its head.*

When the divine world spoke about this topic at the beginning of the 1980s, scientists hardly gave it a second thought. This is again an example of the fact that God gives warning in time, even before scientists know about it. Here we will chronologically offer several excerpts from divine revelations addressing the polar shift. Following that, the scientifically proven facts concerning this – as they are known until 2008.

Brother Emanuel, the cherub of divine Wisdom, said to humankind in 1980:

... I say to you, there will be a colossal change in the poles and unending suffering will break in over this earth.

In 1984, Christ said to us human beings:

... polar shifts are indicated, whereby the oceans rise out of their beds and seek other basins ...

In 1992, Christ pointed out the following:

The earth is rebelling from the many causes that are now coming into effect more and more. But the great of this world have long since not understood this. They are steering the nations into the greatest disaster, namely, a polar shift, such as never before happened.

Oh see: I, Christ, still hold in My hands the earth's magnetic field, the mighty dynamo for this earth, which radiates into the All, to the stars and planets, and which establishes the connection to the cosmos, the All. And so, I still hold this dynamo in My hands, but the causes are pressing more and more to come into effect. This means that the earth's magnetic field must slip out of My hands through the law of cause and effect, because the people with their hunger and striving for power want it this way. This means that everything is over in an instant. Then man will experience what is written in the stars: What he sent into space will fall back down on the earth. All the rubbish of technology will fall onto the earth and thus onto the people, as if the stars were to fall from heaven.

Verily I say to you, then the waters will come and cover over the rubbish and the great transformation will take place ever more, from the negative to the positive.

Christ spoke further in this revelation about the consequences of this event:

> *When the dynamo of this earth collapses, there will be even greater suffering on the earth, because people, animals, plants and stones are connected to the dynamo. ... During this time, the living will envy the dead, and they will call: "Death, you sweet one, where are you?" For there will be hardly any energies that help the person to heal his physical body, to restore his physical body.*

And two months later, Christ revealed through Gabriele:

> *The light of God in Me, the Christ, is calling you to turn back and change your ways. You can no longer solve this global problem, and nothing at all is solved. There are many ostensible solutions, but only ostensible – and nothing is solved. It will be solved through worldwide disasters. This potential of sin that the earth has to bear will be covered up by the great flood, for a mighty polar shift will cover up everything human and the stars that form anew will purify the earth and raise it up, so that on earth can emerge what has already now begun: the Kingdom of Peace of Jesus Christ, My kingdom, in which I Am the ruler.*

Christ continued in His message from the All:

> *I spoke of a mighty polar shift. Smaller things are preceding this. The one who looks into world events and at the earth recognizes what is looming and feels the shake-ups that are indicating it." (Christ-Radiation, Apr. 1, 1992)*

It took a relatively long time until science turned its attention to the planet earth, to its magnetic field and the changes in it.

However, today more and more scientific evidence is accumulating that points to an impending reversal of the poles.

- According to present geophysical knowledge, there are two main sources for the earth's magnetic field. The so-called inner field, whose source lies within the earth's core, supplies 98% of the measurable strength of the magnetic field. 2% comes from the external field, which is based on electric currents in the ionosphere and magnetosphere. It is known that an electric field induces a magnetic field and vice versa.[141]

Basically, the earth consists of four layers: The earth's crust, on which we live, the earth's mantle, as well as the outer and inner core of the earth. The outer core consists mainly of liquid iron and nickel and exists at depths of 2900 to 5150 km within the earth. Beneath this is the inner core, which extends to the earth's center at a depth of 6370 km. It also consists largely of iron, which however, is solid because of the enormous pressures there. The inner core is about 1000 degrees warmer than the outer core and heats up the liquid iron in the outer core like a stove burner. Vortexes and turbulences develop in the liquid iron, which in combination with the earth's rotation produce a mechanical energy, which then transforms into electrical energy, thus inducing a magnetic field. This geodynamic principle has in the meantime been proven experimentally. For about 150 years, an increasing reduction of the magnetic field has been observed. According to researchers at a meeting of the American Geophysical Union, the magnetic field has weakened 10% since the 19th century. Recent data indicates that the strength of the magnetic field is presently decreasing about 6.6 % per century. Since 1979, a decrease of 1.7% has been determined. However, there are regions where the earth's magnetic field is decreasing faster than average. Over the South Atlantic between Cape Town and Buenos Aires, the decrease is 100 times faster than normal. From data collected by the Danish satellite Oersted, it can be observed that the magnetic field in the South Atlantic and at the North Pole has already reversed.

This means that these regions are working like a kind of anti-dynamo. The magnetic field of this anti-dynamo exists at the same time next to the normal magnetic field. Since a very fast growth of this anti-dynamo has been observed, this could lead to a reversal of the earth's magnetic field within a short period of time. For this, the balance between the anti-dynamo and the dynamo have only to be transposed. Computer simulations show that such anti-dynamos play an important role in a complete polar reversal.

The South Atlantic Anomaly leads to the occurrence of strong highly energetic cosmic radiation there. The space station ISS 90 receives 90% of its dangerous radiation in the South Atlantic region even though it is there only 10 minutes per day. Because electronic breakdowns and other damages have repeatedly occurred over the South Atlantic region, satellites are now programmed to avoid the region. What can be observed in addition is an increasingly rapid movement of the magnetic North Pole. It presently lies between northeastern Canada and Greenland and is now traveling 40 kilometers per year. It is estimated that it will reach Siberia by the year 2050.

A reversal of the earth's magnetic field has taken place many times during the course of the earth's history. This can be observed in the magnetic orientation of the volcanic rock on both sides of the mid-oceanic ridges. In this region of the ocean floor, magma is continually erupting, which as it cools, freezes, so to speak, the polarization of the current field.

A reversal of the earth's magnetic field has occurred every 300,000 years on the average.
The last time was about 780,000 years ago, indicating that a reversal of the poles may be long overdue.

There are only sparse scientific indications of the consequences a polar shift will have. It has been assumed that for many centuries there will be a very weak, chaotic magnetic field with several poles. Anomalies in the magnetic field will certainly affect animal species that orient themselves by magnetic fields. For example, it is known that whales are often stranded on coastal areas where magnetic valleys exist.

Based on present data about the influence of the earth's magnetic field on humans, there will probably be disturbances in heart function and an increased occurrence of psychiatric illnesses. It is a well-known fact that the earth's magnetic field forms a protective shield against highly energetic radiation from space. Solar flares and their resulting magnetic storms could disturb the supply of electricity in many regions of the earth (the last one took place in Quebec Province, in Canada, 1989). Various scientists assume that the solar wind will form a protective layer around the earth when the magnetic field collapses. In scientific publications to date,

113

no great concern on the part of geophysicists and astronomers can be found.

We leave it to our readers to decide whether to rely on the statements of geophysicists and astronomers, or – after all that has been pointed out in this book – to take seriously the warnings from God.

In the Christ-revelation about cause and effect in 1980, cited at the beginning of this book, Christ spoke about the significance of the earth's magnetic field for human beings, animals and nature. He then compared the earth with a human being and called the planet the "earth-man." He said:

Now, among other things, I'm talking about the garment of the great earth-man. The garment consists of the realm of minerals, nature and animals. The magnetic fields of the earth-man are the nerve centers; the earth's magnetic currents are the pathways of the nerves.

This image of the magnetic fields described as the earth's nerve centers is very graphic. In humans and, of course, in animals, the nerves are responsible for transmitting stimuli. When we think of all that man does to the planet Earth, we can imagine what "stress" the "earth-man" is constantly exposed to.

In a revelation from 1986, which one can read in the book "Cause and Development of All Illness,"[142] Christ explained the interaction between humans and the earth's magnetic field. There it says on page 66:

A person is a bundle of energy that, according to his thinking and acting, creates its own fields of energy, or magnetic fields. Therefore, every person has his own

*energetic and magnetic fields, which correspond to his
way of thinking and acting.*

*There is continual interaction between his magnetic fields
and the magnetic fields of the earth: The reactions of the
earth are relayed to the human being through the
interaction between human being and earth, just as the
actions of people are relayed to the vibration of the earth.
Whatever a person does to his earth, his dwelling planet,
he does to himself because of this interaction between
man and earth.*

So here we again find the law of cause and effect. What a
person does to the earth he ultimately does to himself. We
continue in the book on pages 66-67:

*The magnetic fields of the earth register all the actions of
the inhabitants of the earth, the human beings. And the
magnetic streams – which are the sound-carriers of the
great "earth-man," the earth – bring all resonances, no
matter what their fallout, whether positive or negative,
back to the one who emitted them: the human being …*

*The earth's magnetic fields register every dissonance,
especially the human acts of violence which provoke
considerable atmospheric disturbances as well as
disruptions in and on the earth, for instance, by nuclear
tests and the like. All dissonances are transmitted by the
magnetic streams, the sound-carriers of the earth's
magnetic fields, which may also be figuratively called the
nerves of the earth.*

*The magnetic fields of the earth are ranges of varying
frequencies which, in their entirety, are called the earth's
magnetic field. They are the "nerve points" of the earth,
and at the same time, the mirrors of the dwelling planet.*

If these mirrors of the earth are altered and dulled by man's wrong doing, then this has an effect on the entire earth: on the climate, on the nature kingdoms and on human beings. The magnetic streams even change the behavioral patterns of the animals.

In this book "Cause and Development of All Illness" from 1986, many more interconnections are addressed that are far beyond the present state of knowledge in science.

The Murder of Animals Is the Death of Humans

In a divine message from the year 1980, Christ explained not only the relationship between the earth's magnetic field and humans, He also explained the following:

The eternal life of God streams through all life forms, through the organs of the earth-man, through the garment. When man now acts against this earth-man, at the same time he is acting against his own life. If man only knew that as soon as he violates an animal, he is harming his own body, by shadowing his soul and reducing the inner strength, the spirit-power! The unknowing person steps and acts thoughtlessly on this great earth-man! He intentionally and unintentionally destroys the realms of nature and of the animals!

Oh see! Animals are bred and raised for slaughter. The preceding thoughts to this are based on the unlawful word "death" – killing for meat to eat. Again, man is acting against the great law of God. He opposes the commandment "You shall not kill!" This also applies to the great earth-

116

man, to this earth. Everything that happens willfully penetrates your soul and burdens it. In this way, man is continually destroying this earth. He is damaging the great earth-man and does not think more about the fact that this great earth-man will one day defend himself. ...

We human beings are destroying the earth with factory farming. Scientists have meanwhile researched these interconnections and it is becoming ever more clear what ecological consequences the wanton killing of animals for consumption has for the earth and ultimately for humankind. Most people are not aware that a mass killing of 45 billion animals for human consumption takes place every year.

Most of the facts in the following section can be found in a report published in November 2006 by the Food and Agriculture Organization of the United Nations entitled "Livestock's Long Shadow." [143]

- Altogether twice as many slaughter animals as people live on the earth. 49% of the grain harvest and 90% of the world soybean harvest is used to fatten up these animals. Livestock production takes up 70% of the total area of land used for agriculture and 30% of the land surface of this planet. This is one of the main reasons for hunger in the world.

- Livestock production accounts for 8% of global water use, primarily for the production of feed. 15,000 liters of water are needed to produce one kilo of beefsteak. In contrast, 1500 liters are needed to grow one kilo of wheat, while a human being needs 2.5 liters of drinking water per day.

700 scientists conducted a study on the topic of fresh water supply (Comprehensive Assessment of Water Management in Agriculture) and concluded that the most effective way to save water is to avoid eating meat.[144]

- Livestock is probably the greatest cause of water pollution and contributes to the over-fertilization of coastal waters, to the development of so-called dead zones and to the destruction of coral reefs. It contributes one third of the pollution of freshwater with nitrogen and phosphate. 50% of the water pollution in Europe is caused by factory farming. In the USA, agriculture's share of water pollution is greater than that of all cities and industries combined.

- 15 kilos of manure slurry are the result of the production of one kilo pork – in Germany 66 million tons annually. In the USA the environmental pollution caused by the feces from animal factories is 130 times higher than the pollution caused by human beings.

- The expansion of livestock production is a key factor in the deforestation of the rainforests. 70% of the deforested regions in the Amazon basin are now used for pasturing animals; growing animal feed takes most of the rest. Altogether, 90% of the destruction of tropical rainforests is the result of factory farming.

- Livestock production has a share of 18% of CO_2 equivalents in the greenhouse effect. Every cow produces up to 250 liters of methane per day; worldwide this amounts to 300 billion liters. Billions of sheep and goats raise the global methane emission to circa 150 trillion liters per year. All in all, according to calculations made by the FAO, cattle production burdens the climate about as severely as do all the people in India, Germany and Japan together. If sheep, goats and pigs, poultry and the production of animal feed are calculated in, this results in a figure that nearly corresponds to the share of the USA in global climate damage. According to the study published by the FAO in 2006, livestock production damages the climate more than all means of transportation in the world.

- According to the opinion of the Marburg, Germany researcher Ralf Conrad, managing director of the Max-Planck Institute for Terrestrial Microbiology, the climate change could be slowed down if people would eat differently. "In a nutshell, the motto could be: Eat no more beef; forego milk products."

The methane produced by the bacteria in the stomachs of ruminants is one of the strongest greenhouse gases. To turn the "methane screw" in the atmosphere could have a positive effect faster than to want to reduce CO_2 emissions, said Conrad. "The methane circulation in the atmosphere can be influenced within circa 8 years; while carbon dioxide will take decades."[145]

- The oceans could be fished empty by 2148. Considering the increasing environmental pollution and the over fishing of the oceans, scientists fear a collapse of life in rivers, lakes and oceans by 2048. Should the present trend continue, nearly all species of fish and crustaceans will be extinct by approximately the middle of the century. This would threaten the balance of the entire ecosystem, as Boris Worm of the Dalhousie University in Halifax, Nova Scotia put it.[146]

These are only some of the facts regarding the ecological disasters that are caused by the consumption of meat. But the murder of animals leads not only indirectly to the death of many people, the killing of animals and the consumption of meat have further consequences.

Even though no person can create life, he takes the right for himself to take the lives of other forms of life. But "What is life?" – Christ answered this question in a message from the All in 1980. He spoke through Gabriele:

Man violates life day after day. What is life? It pulsates not only in man, but in all life forms. Oh see, the law of cause and effect is taking place in your souls. Whoever acts against the life of nature, of the animal and mineral realms is also burdening his soul. ...

And Christ also explained:

The wanton killing of animals and the excessive eating of meat creates causes that also fall back on your souls. Humankind wears furs and leather! Do you not know that everything is vibration, that an animal's fear is also vibration? You eat meat and kill the animals for this. You go hunting and kill for your own sake. Have you ever thought about how they suffer, what feelings of fear the animals have in their inner being? I say to you that all these feelings of the animals not only penetrate the organs, the skin, the fur – but also they penetrate the flesh. The person partakes of this flesh with great relish. The animal's fear vibrates in this prepared food; it is a low vibration. How can person and soul come into a high vibration when the person kills for his own sake? The vibration of fear clings to the leather as well as to your furs. This fear transfers itself and continues to exist, even when the leather is tanned ever so often.

Again and again, the divine world has addressed the fact that everything that man does to the animals will fall back on him again. Since 1989, the following clear words can be read by all people in the great work of revelation "This Is My Word" on page 211:

Recognize furthermore that the suffering of animals and the consumed flesh of the animals that have been deliberately killed gnaw, in turn, at the flesh of the person. The consequences are disease and pestilence. They are the effects of these and similar causes.

The large number of diseases that are fostered by eating meat can be mentioned here only briefly. However, you can read much more about this in the booklet "Vegetarisch essen – Fleisch vergessen. Ärztlicher Ratgeber für Vegetarier und Veganer."[147]

- The consumption of meat, sausage, fish and poultry is a risk factor for numerous diseases such as diabetes and gout. Meat promotes excess weight and resulting heart and circulatory diseases, stroke and circulatary problems, among other things. Meat harms the bones, thus raising the risk for osteoporosis and bone fractures. Meat is a risk factor for cancer. Meat promotes inflammation and pain. Meat fosters heart attacks and arteriosclerosis.

- Many environmental poisons, in particular, are found in meat; for example, 90% of all dioxins and furans are absorbed via animal foods.

- Briefly summarized, we can say that vegetarians not only live healthier, but also longer! This was the conclusion of a study by the German Cancer Research Center.

When we read this, then it becomes clear what Christ meant when He said:
The suffering of animals and the consumed flesh of the animals that have been deliberately killed gnaw, in turn, at the flesh of the person. The consequences are disease and pestilence.

- People must brace themselves for new infectious diseases: Particularly in Latin America, tropical Africa and South Asia, new fatal plagues such as HIV, SARS or Ebola could emerge in the future, which could hit the local population and, in the course of globalization, all people. This was determined by a research team working with Kate Jones of the Zoological Society of London.
  The researchers studied 335 infectious diseases that have emerged in the world since 1940. In 60% of the cases, so-called zoonoses were involved; these are infectious diseases that have crossed over from animals to humans. Over the decades between 1940 and the present, there has been a rising trend of new infectious diseases. According to the conclusions of researchers, the greatest danger for cross-over diseases is where animals are crowded into ever-smaller areas, while man spreads out more and more.[148]

- A disease that is transmitted to humans by the consumption of meat is the Mad Cow Disease. The prions, which are found in muscle meat and milk, which until recently were classified as harmless, could lead to the Creutzfeld-Jakob Disease in humans. Like Morbus Alzheimer, this disease is one of the neuro-degenerative diseases that cannot always be clearly differentiated from each other by means of their clinical symptoms. The number of people who died of Morbus Alzheimer's in the USA increased 50-fold between 1979 and 2000. However, no one can specifically estimate how many actually had Alzheimer's Disease and how many in reality died of CJD.[149]

- Mad Cow Disease (bovine spongiform encephalopathy [BSE]) is related to the scrapie disease in sheep. French researchers found the pathogen of BSE-related scrapie in the muscle flesh of sheep long before the animals showed signs of illness. With this, the presence of prions was first shown to exist in the muscle meat of an animal that is eaten by humans. ...[150]

Apparently people don't even realize how many illnesses they actually get by eating meat, since most people prefer to cling to the present state of science – which is usually very quickly outdated – than to listen to the word of God through the mouth of a prophet.

- Another pestilence from the animal kingdom is bird flu. Dutch researchers now want to attempt combining the Asiatic bird flu pathogen and a human influenza pathogen into a new virus, in order to clarify how dangerous such a combination of the two flu viruses could be. WHO has warned for a long time about a pandemic that could result from this. In this connection, the Spanish influenza is referred to again and again, which killed between 20 and

40 million people between 1918 and 1920.[151] US agencies are already preparing for such a global pandemic.

In 1980, Christ already gave warning about killing animals for consumption. In 1981, American scientists described the clinical symptoms of AIDS for the first time.

- Approximately 25 million people have died worldwide from this immune-deficiency disease.[152] Researchers think that the AIDS pathogen HIV developed in apes from various forms of SIV and was then transferred to humans.[153] They fear that this mechanism could be repeated. In Cameroon, however, there have been people with AIDS symptoms who tested negative for the AIDS pathogen HIV as well as the ape variety SIV …[154]
  For the first time, in 2004, the transmission of the simian foamy virus, another ape disease, to game hunters was reported. Even though the hunters have not yet developed any symptoms, experts fear the development of a new disease.[155]

AIDS was transferred to humans by the consumption of monkey meat. Particularly the consumption of wild animals can lead to terrible illnesses in humans, for Ebola and SARS were most likely also transmitted to humans through the consumption of wild animals. However, it is not only in Africa or Asia that wild animals are eaten. Approximately 5 million wild animals were killed in Germany last year, many of them for consumption.

At the end of this chapter we would like to pass on a question of the Creator-Spirit, which He asked people through Gabriele in 1997:

Many of you say that animals have infectious diseases. Who infected them – God or humans? You take in this information and experience the infectious diseases on your physical body. Who is to blame? God? Or you, yourselves?

The Future

"The Murder of Animals Is the Death of Humans" is the title of the 16th issue from the series "The Prophet,"[156] in which still many more facts on this topic can be found:

In this pamphlet there is an excerpt from a revelation of God from the year 1999. The Eternal One spoke to humankind:

It is enough with the excesses of human wickedness, with the crimes against the provider of man, against Mother Earth!

The wretched creatures who think that they could out-trump the Creator will soon have to realize that Mother Earth no longer obeys them. The earth is now Mine and will do what is My Will. This means that the causes, the transgressions of the people against the Mother Earth will come over them as effects ever more quickly.

What these words of the Eternal mean has already become unavoidable reality. Even science makes forecasts for the future:

- Long-term statistics demonstrate that the number of large natural disasters rose dramatically during the 2nd half of the 20th century. During the 1950s, there were about 20 great disasters per year. By the 1990s, this number had risen to 90.[157] This trend is continuing rapidly at the beginning of the 21st century. In particular, it is reckoned that there will be a rapid increase in weather disasters.

• According to studies by the Munich Reinsurance Society, the economic damages caused by natural disasters have multiplied eight-fold; the insured damages have risen even more, reflecting a 15-fold increase.[158]

This situation clearly points out that it is as God-Father said it would be: The causes of man are coming into effect ever faster. The culmination, which may be the tipping point, has been reached. Humankind listened neither to the great prophets of God of the Old Testament nor to Jesus of Nazareth or the enlightened men and women who came after Him, so that now, what Christ revealed already in 1984 is becoming visible:

Verily, verily, I announced this time as Jesus of Nazareth. And this time was announced over and over again through the mouth of a prophet. Christ – I, the Inner Light – wanted to stand by every single person, every single soul. My wish and My will was and is that humankind turn to the inner stream, the holy power, and not violate the earth, not arm itself, and not cultivate hostility, but friendship and love. And so I ask humankind: Who is able to cleanse the oceans, cleanse and stabilize the cycles of the earth? Who is able to stop volcanic activity? Who is able to heal the continuous emergence of diseases and pestilences? Who can cleanse the earth? Who can refashion this dwelling planet, as God gave it to His human children? Is it possible that man alone can bring all this about? No! The causes that have been set will come into effect – and they will show themselves soon!

Look into this world! In all places, you can see how humankind behaves!

Diseases, needs and worries, unemployment and much more are the order of the day! So many are calling: "Where is Christ?" Oh recognize: A great era has dawned! Christ, the Inner Light, has set out again to call humankind and say to each and every one: You are the temple of the Holy Spirit! Save your soul from darkness and imprisonment, from spiritual blindness! Awaken, O man, and repent, for the time is near when such things will happen!

What will happen was revealed by God, the Eternal, through Gabriele on Feb. 27, 2001, in a serious and grave message, which at that time was broadcast all over the world in many languages via many radio stations. To conclude, you may now read these words of the Creator. In this way, no person can say that he did not know.

The Creator spoke:
I AM the God of Abraham, the God of Isaac and the God of Jacob. I Am the God of all true prophets.
I, God, the Almighty, raise My voice through My prophetess and spiritual ambassador, and direct it to all humankind.

Stop consuming your fellow creatures, which are your animal brothers and sisters!
Stop torturing them in animal experiments and taking away their freedom by keeping them in barns and pens which are unworthy of them. Animals love freedom just as you, the human beings.

Stop killing the tiniest of animals, the microscopic life of the soil, through artificial fertilizers, and excrements and the like!

Stop cutting and burning down the forests and taking the habitat of animals away from them in forests and fields. Give them back their living space, the forests, fields and meadows; otherwise, your fate, which you have inflicted upon yourselves, will take away your house and home and your sources of food, through worldwide catastrophes which you have created yourselves through your behavior against the life, against the kingdoms of nature, including the animals.

Should human beings again toss My words to the wind, the storm, the fate that is worldwide, will begin and sweep away the people by the hundreds of thousands – on the one hand through worldwide catastrophes, on the other, through illnesses which break in over them like the epidemics which, by turning their backs on every kind of spiritual ethics and morals, they have inflicted on the animals that they are presently burning by the thousands. Similar things will happen to the one who does not turn back and change his ways.

My word is spoken. The worldwide apocalypse is underway. The one who does not want to hear this, will feel his created causes as effects at ever shorter intervals. I have raised the earth with its plants, animals and minerals to Me. The one who continues to raise his hands against Mother Earth with all her forms of life will feel the effects. Stop torturing, killing and murdering!

You human beings, stop with your bestial behavior, which only hits back at you and no other being; for what you do to the least of your fellow creatures, you do to Me and to yourself.

It is enough! Change your ways, otherwise the harvest, which is your seed, will move forward.

I AM the I AM, always the same, yesterday, today and tomorrow, in all eternity.

All those who have read these divine words of revelation with heart and mind should have an inkling of the future of this world. But each one of us determines the future of the individual person himself, for we are the architects of our fate. Already in 1989, Brother Emanuel pointed out the following:

This world, in its present state, can no longer be saved. The soul and the person can be saved, but here, too, let it be said: Save yourselves, you who want to be saved. I deliberately put value on the word "want," for the rescue is Christ alone, who is in each one of you, the Redeemer-force that makes you free.

In His care and love, the Spirit of the Christ of God has thrown us a life ring countless times through Gabriele, so that every seeking and willing person can leave the sinking world-ship, to find security and a hold in Christ.

If you like, and with these thoughts in mind, we invite you, dear reader, to consider the words of our brother and Redeemer, Christ, from the year 1992:

I, the Christ of God, call all people to turn back and change their ways. To turn back means to go into the inner life, for the Kingdom of God is in each one of you as strength and light. Deep in your inner being, each one of you is a being from God, which I, Christ, through My Redeemer-deed, lead back to the primordial stream of life, to God. For this reason, I call upon all people to take the path to the inner life. A person attains the inner life by actualizing the commandments of life and by applying the Sermon on the Mount in his life. Then he establishes communication with the inner life and can be protected by the kingdom of life, by the inner kingdom. ...

You people of this earth, now it is no longer: Save your body. Now it is: Save your soul, so that your body can be protected, if it is good for soul and body. You people of this earth, I repeat: Now it is, "Save your souls!" And the Savior Am I, Christ, your Redeemer.

Do not ask where I Am. Do not seek Me here and there. I Am the Spirit of life in God, your Father and Mine. The Spirit of life dwells in your souls. You can find Me there. For this reason, take the path to life, to the Savior, to within. And so, the person must turn back and go within, by actualizing more and more the commandments of life, the Ten Commandments, and by including the Sermon on the Mount in his life. In this way, the person will gain entry to the inner life, to the Christ of God, who I Am in each one of you as strength and light.

And so, it is no longer, "Save your physical body." Save your soul! And there is only one Savior: It is I, Christ, in God, your Father and Mine. Where do you seek Me? Where will you find Me? Not in external trumpery. This is coming to an end. Only in you, yourself, Am I the life, the Savior. You will find Me by taking the path within, to the kingdom of the inner life; for the Kingdom of God is within, in you.

So note well: Each one of you is the temple of the Holy Spirit. The one who cleanses this temple sanctifies this temple and finds access to the inner life, which I Am. All outer temples – no matter what they are called – will pass away. They will fall victim to the transformation. The earth will become a fallow land, so that it will be able to draw new life from itself. ...

You people of this earth, receive My peace and My salvation once more. Remember, I Am the only Savior. You do not need to seek Me here and there – you will find Me in your inner being, because each one of you is the temple, in which salvation dwells. Cleanse the temple, sanctify the temple – and you will find yourselves in the kingdom of the inner being, to which I, Christ, the Son of the All-Highest, belong and to which you belong. For deep in your inner beings, you are children of the eternal kingdom.

I brought you My peace, and I leave you My peace. Peace.

Endnotes

[1] *ZENIT* (news agency reporting mainly on the Holy See), Jan. 21, 2005: http://www.zenit.org/german/visualizza.phtml?sid=65094

[2] *WDR Nachtrichten*, (West German Broadcasting Co. News) Jan. 7, 2005.

[3] *N24 Nachtrichten, AP*, Jan. 6, 2005: http://www.jiggle.de/vb/archive/index.php/t-24463.html

[4] Luther Deutsch, *die Werke Martin Luther in neuer Auswahl für die Gegenwart,* published by Kurt Aland, Vol. 9: *Tischreden*, 3rd, fully newly revised edition, Stuttgart 1960; Reclam-edition, Ditzingen 1987, p. 672.

[5] *Kath.net*, Dec. 31, 2004: http://www.kath.net/detail.php?id=9331

[6] Deschner, Karlheinz, *Die beleidigte Kirche oder: Wer stört den öffentlichen Frieden?...* Freiburg: Ahriman, January 1986.

[7] *Second Council of Constantinople in 553:*
11. If anyone does not anathematize Arius, Eunomius, Macedonius, Apollinarius Nestorius, Eutyches and Origen, as well as their heretical books, and also all other heretics who have already been condemned and anathematized by the holy, catholic and apostolic church and by the four holy synods which have already been mentioned, and also all those who have thought or now think in the same way as the aforesaid heretics and who persist in their error even to death: let him be anathema.
Norman P. Tanner, ed., *Decrees of the Ecumenical Councils.*

[8] *Gesundheit.de*: http://www.gesundheit.de/krankheiten/infektionskrankheiten/index.html

[9] *Ärzte Zeitung*, July 14, 2004:
http://www.aerztezeitung.de/docs/2004/07/14/130a0203.asp?npro.

[10] *World Health Organization Report 2007*:
http://whqlibdoc.who.int/publications/2007/9789241563141_eng.pdf

[11] *WHO Fact Sheet No. 267*, revised 2005:
http://www.who.int/mediacentre/factsheets/fs267/en/index.html

[12] *WHO Fact Sheet No. 115*, revised May 2008:
http://www.who.int/mediacentre/factsheets/fs117/en/

[13] *WHO Fact Sheet No. 94*, May 2007:
http://www.who.int/mediacentre/factsheets/fs094/en/index.html

[14] *UNAIDS, 2007 UN Epidemic Update*:
http://www.unaids.org/en/KnowledgeCentre/HIVData/EpiUpdate/EpiUpdArchive/2007/

[15] *MDR* (Central German Broadcasting Co.) Jan. 31, 2004:
http://www.mdr.de/hauptsache-gesund/105664.html
See also: *WHO Fact Sheet No. 204*, August 2008:
http://www.who.int/mediacentre/factsheets/fs204/en/index.html

[16] *Reuters*, Dec. 11, 2003:
http://www.commondreams.org/headlines03/1211-13.htm
See also *WHO Fact Sheet: Climate and Health*, July 2005:
http://www.who.int/globalchange/news/fsclimandhealth/en/index.html

[17] *Reuters*, Nov. 25, 2007:
http://www.reuters.com/article/environmentNews/idUSL2518480220071125?feedType=RSS &feedName=environmentNews

[18] *National Geographic News*, Dec. 12, 2007:
http://news.nationalgeographic.com/news/2007/12/071212-AP-arctic-melt.html

[19] *Spiegel Online*, Feb. 19, 2008:
http://www.igsoc.org/journal/54/184/j07j061.pdf

[20] *Spiegel.de*, Mar. 24, 2006:
http://www.spiegel.de/wissenschaft/natur/0,1518,407603,00.html
Refers to article in "Science," 25 Aug. 2006, vol. 313, no. 5790.
pp.1043-1045.

[21] See: http://de.wikipedia.org/wiki/Meeresspiegelanstieg
Extensive info, but not these exact figures under:
http://en.wikipedia.org/wiki/Sea_level_rise

[22] *The Independent*, Jan. 14, 2008:
http://www.independent.co.uk/environment/climate-change/loss-of-
antarctic-ice-has-soared-by-75-per-cent-in-just-10-years-
769894.html

[23] *Science Daily*, Jan. 22, 2008:
http://www.sciencedaily.com/releases/2008/01/080120160720.htm

[24] *Süddeutsche Zeitung*, Mar. 11, 2008:
http://www.sueddeutsche.de/wissen/artikel/351/162897/

[25] *Scinexx*, Nov. 11, 2007:
http://www.g-o.de/wissen-aktuell-7417-2007-11-20.html

[26] *FAZ.NET*:
http://www.faz.net/s/RubC5406E1142284FB6BB79CE
581A20766E/Doc~EF126C667F9394469996118AD2A8E8A
3E~ATpl~Ecommon~ Scontent.html
Refers to articles by: Tom Wigley (US climate researcher, was on
IPCC) in *Nature*, No. 452, pp. 531-531, 3 April 2008.
Damon Matthews (Concordia University, Montreal) & Ken Caldeira
(Carnegie Institute, Stanford, CA) in *Geophysical Research Letters*,
Mar. 7, 2008:
http://www.scitizen.com/screens/blogPage/viewBlog/
sw_viewBlog.php?idTheme=13&idContribution=1495

[27] http://www.unisdr.org/disaster-statistics/introduction.htm

[28] *Welt Mobil*, Jan. 24, 2008:
http://www71.sevenval-fit.com/welt/deeplink/welt/politik/article1576996/Naturkatastrophen durch Klimawandel verdoppelt.xmli

See also:
http://www.monstersandcritics.com/science/nature/news/article 1380625.phpRed Cross reports growing rates of natural disasters

[29] *ORF* (Austrian Broadcasting Co.):
science.orf.at/science/news/106878

[30] *New Scientist*, Sept. 26, 2006:
http://www.newscientist.com/article/dn10159-global-warming-nears-a-millionyear-high.html

[31] *ORF*:
science.orf.at/science/news/113684
Refers to online article of *Science* magazine, May 13, 2004.

[32] *NASA*, Oct. 19, 2006:
http://www.nasa.gov/vision/earth/lookingatearth/ozone record.html

[33] *ORF*, June 2005:
science.orf.at/science/news/115477

[34] *Kurier*, Jan. 18, 2008:
http://www.kurier.at/nachrichten/122996.php

[35] *OEDC*, Dec. 4, 2007:
http://www.oecd.org/document/34/0,3343,en 2649 201185 3972 7650 1 1 1 1,00.html

[36] *IIED*, Mar. 28, 2003:
http://www.iied.org/general/media/archive-media/climate-change-study-maps-those-greatest-risk-cyclones-and-rising-seas-0

[37] *Scripps News*, Feb. 17, 2005:
http://scrippsnews.ucsd.edu/Releases/?releaseID=666

[38] *ORF,* Feb. 18, 2005:
http://science.orf.at/science/news/132827
Science, June 17, 2005, Vol. 308, No. 5729, pp. 1772-1774.
Abstract: http://www.sciencemag.org/cgi/content/full/308/5729/1772

[39] *Nature,* Dec. 18, 2003, Vol. 426, pp. 826-829.
Abstract: http://www.nature.com/nature/journal/v426/n6968/full/nature02206.html

[40] *Spiegel-Online,* Mar. 16, 2008:
http://www.spiegel.de/wissenschaft/natur/0,1518,541817,00.html

[41] *Umwelt Bundes Amt,* August 2006:
http://www.raonline.ch/pages/edu/pdf3/umweltde_permafrost1106.pdf
See also:
http://en.wikipedia.org/wiki/Effects_of_global_warming#Methane_release_from_melting_permafrost_peat_bogs

[42] *Spiegel Online,* Sept. 7, 2006:
http://www.spiegel.de/wissenschaft/natur/0,1518,435766,00.html

[43] *Spiegel-Online International,* Apr. 17, 2008:
http://www.spiegel.de/international/world/0,1518,547976,00.html

[44] *Focus Online,* Oct. 24, 2007:
http://www.focus.de/wissen/wissenschaftklimawandel_aid_136923.html
See also:
Proceedings of the Royal Society B: Biological Sciences, Vol. 275, No. 1630, Jan. 7, 2008.

[45] *Netzeitung.de,* July 16, 2004:
http://www.netzeitung.de/spezial/klimawandel/296012.html

[46] *Focus Online,* Jan. 18, 2008:
http://www.focus.de/wissen/wissenschaft/odenwalds_universum/odenwalds-universum_aid_233387.html

[47] *Informationsdienst Wissenschaft,* July 27, 2007:
Cited from: *Zenk, W.* and *E. Morozov,* 2007:
"Decadal Warming of the Coldest Antarctic Bottom Water Flow through the Vema Channel." Geophysical Research Letters, 34, L14607, doi: 10.1029/2007GL030340.
http://www.agu.org/pubs/crossref/2007/2007GL030340.shtml

[48] *Swiss Re:* "Storm Damage in Europe on the Rise":
http://www.swissre.com/resources/0e9e8a80455c7a86b1e4bb80a45d76a0-Publ06_Klimaveraenderung_en.pdf

[49] *Spiegel Online,* Dec. 31, 2007:
http://www.spiegel.de/panorama/0,1518,525742,00.html

[50] *WWF News,* March 2, 2006. Complete report:
http://www.wwf.org.uk/filelibrary/pdf/stormyeuropereport.pdf

[51] *USA Today,* June 7, 2007:
http://www.usatoday.com/weather/hurricane/2007-06-07-cyclone-gonu_N.htm

[52] http://en.wikipedia.org/wiki/Timeline_of_the_2007_Atlantic_hurri cane_season

[53] *USA Today,* Sept. 15, 2005:
http://www.usatoday.com/weather/climate/2005-09-15-globalwarming-hurricanes_x.htm

[54] http://en.wikipedia.org/wiki/2005_Atlantic_hurricane_season

[55] Inge Niedek and Harald Frater, *"Naturkatastrophen, Wirbelstürme, Beben, Vulkanausbrüche..."* Springer Verlag, Berlin Heidelberg, 2004, pp.103-04.
See also:
http://en.wikipedia.org/wiki/Hurricanes

[56] *Ibid.,* pp. 111-112.
See also:
http://en.wikipedia.org/wiki/Tornadoes

[57] *Insurance Journal,* Nov. 23, 2004:
http://www.insurancejournal.com/news/international/2004/11/23/
47953.htm

[58] See: http://en.wikipedia.org/wiki/2004_Indian_Ocean_earthquake

[59] *BBC News,* Dec. 31, 2004:
http://news.bbc.co.uk/1/hi/world/africa/4134485.stm

[60] See: http://en.wikipedia.org/wiki/2004_Indian_Ocean_earthquake

[61] See: http://en.wikipedia.org/wiki/2004_Indian_Ocean_earthquake#
Casualties_in_historical_context

[62] *WWF,* "Wälder in Flammen," March 2007:
http://www.wwf.de/fileadmin/fm-wwf/pdf_neu/wwf_waldbrand
studie.pdf

[63] Keynote address by Josette Sheeran, Executive Director UN World
Food Programme, at Center for Strategic and International Studies,
Washington, DC. April 18, 2008, *"The New Face of Hunger":*
http://documents.wfp.org/stellent/groups/public/documents/
newsroom/wfp177149.pdf

[64] *Deutsche Welthungerhilfe,* "World Hunger Index 2007":
http://www.welthungerhilfe.de/fileadmin/media/pdf/WHI/Bericht
_Welthunger_Index_2007.pdf

[65] *UNDP:*
http://content.undp.org/go/newsroom/2007/november/hdr-clim
atechange-20071127.en
German: http://www.dgvn.de/fileadmin/user_upload/PUBLIKATIO-
NEN/UN_Berichte_HDR/HDR/HDR_2007/PM2-HDR07_USA_
deutsch01.pdf

[66] *World Socialist,* Mar. 29, 2008:
http://www.wsws.org/articles/2008/mar2008/fami-m29.shtml

[67] *Spiegel Online,* Mar. 19, 2008:
http://www.spiegel.de/wissenschaft/natur/0,1518,542456,00.html

[68] *RMX-Forum.de*:
http://www.rmx-forum.de/cgi-bin/index.pl?ST=11931&CP=0&F=
167#newmsg

[69] *International Alert,* Nov. 2007:
http://www.international-alert.org/pdf/A_Climate_Of_Conflict.pdf

[70] *Spiegel Online,* Nov. 8, 2007:
http://www.spiegel.de/wissenschaft/mensch/0,1518,515902,00.html

[71] *Welt Online,* Apr. 15, 2008:
http://www.welt.de/wissenschaft/article1904916/Trinkwasser_Ver
sorgung_aus_den_Bergen_bedroht.html

[72] *Ohio State Research News,* Nov. 6, 2007:
http://researchnews.osu.edu/archive/saltwatr.htm

[73] Similar article: *Circle of Blue, Water News,* June 24, 2008:
http://www.circleofblue.org/waternews/world/vanishing-lake-chad-
a-water-crisis-in-central-africa/

[74] Quote: *Welt.de*, July 2, 2007. Article: *PNAS*, July 24, 2007:
http://biology.queensu.ca/~pearl2/SmolandDouglasPNAS2007.pdf

[75] Similar information: http://en.wikipedia.org/wiki/Aral_Sea

[76] More information: *Wikipedia*: http://en.wikipedia.org/wiki/
Aquifers

[77] Similar information: *Unesco*, International Year of Fresh Water, 2003:
http://www.unesco.org/water/iyfw2/ecosystems.shtml

[78] *Suddeutche Zeitung*, Oct. 25, 2007. Press release in English:
United Nations Environmental Program:
http://www.unep.org/Documents.Multilingual/Default.asp?l=en&
ArticleID=5688&DocumentID=519

[79] *Suddeutsche Zeitung*, June 28, 2007:
http://www.sueddeutsche.de/wissen/artikel/909/120756/
See also: *UN News Centre*, June 28, 2007:
http://www.un.org/apps/news/story.asp?NewsID=23073&Cr=deserti
fication&Cr1
See also: http://en.wikipedia.org/wiki/Desertification

[80] *Welt Online*, Sept. 3, 2007:
http://www.welt.de/wissenschaft/article1153528/Wuesten_breiten_sich
_aus_auch_in_Europa.html
See also: *Reuters*, Apr. 4, 2007:
http://www.reuters.com/article/latestCrisis/idUCHI440344

[81] *Scinexx*, Feb. 22, 2002:
http://www.g-o.de/dossier-detail-67-5.html

[82] *IYDD:* http://www.desertifikation.de/ Report in English:
http://www.desertifikation.de/fileadmin/user_upload/downloads/
Desertification_a_security_threat_72dpi.pdf

[83] *Grin Verlag:*
http://www.grin.com/e-book/39473/desertifikation

[84] *Scinexx*, Feb. 22, 2002:
http://www.g-o.de/dossier-detail-67-5.html

[85] *ORF*, Nov. 28, 2007:
http://www.unesco.org/water/iyfw2/ecosystems.shtml
See also: United Nations Development Programme, Nov. 2003:
http://www.undp.org/drylands/docs/land-tenure/workshop-11-05/
Summary_Secure_Access_to_Drylands_Resources(Esther&Stephan).doc

[86] *People's Daily Online*, June 15, 2005:
http://www.ambchine.mu/eng/xwdt/t369657.htm

[87] *ORF*, Nov. 28, 2007:
http://science.orf.at/science/news/150146

[88] Related source: *CSIRO Report*, July 2008:
http://www.csiro.au/resources/MurrayReportMDBSY.html

[89] *Planet Ark,* Oct. 20, 2006:
http://www.planetark.com/avantgo/dailynewsstory.cfm?newsid=38589

[90] *Greenpeace Germany Report,* June 2006:
http://www.greenpeace.de/fileadmin/gpd/user_upload/themen/klima/
greenpeace_wuestenbildung.pdf
See also: http://en.wikipedia.org/wiki/Dust_Bowl

[91] *ORF:*
http://science.orf.at/science/news/13083
Environmental Research Web, Sept. 16, 2008:
http://environmentalresearchweb.org/cws/article/research/35809

[92] *Frankfurter Allgemeine Zeitung,* Apr. 12, 2007:
http://www.faz.net/s/RubCD175863466D41BB9A6A93D460B81174/
Doc~E41072E959F1D4B01B934AD02066AA719~ATpl~Ecommon~
Scontent.html

[93] http://de.wikipedia.org/wiki/Sandsturm

[94] *MSNBC,* Feb. 14, 2008:
http://www.msnbc.msn.com/id/23155918/
Science Magazine, No. 319, p. 948:
http://www.sciencemag.org/cgi/content/abstract/319/5865/948

[95] *Greenpeace Magazine,* 4/00:
http://www.greenpeace-magazin.de/magazinreportage.php?repid=590

[96] J. R. McNeill, *"An Environmental History of the Twentieth-Century
World: Something New Under the Sun."* W.W. Norton & Company,
Inc., New York, 2000, pp. 343-344.

[97] *This Is My Word,* 2nd ed., 1996, Verlag Das Wort, Marktheidenfeld,
Germany.

[98] *Spiegel Online,* Feb. 2, 2008, p. 122:
http://www.spiegel.de/spiegel/0,1518,533229,00.html
Also: *The Independent,* Feb. 5, 2008:
http://www.independent.co.uk/environment/the-worlds-rubbish-dum
p-a-garbage-tip-that-stretches-from-hawaii-to-japan-778016.html

[99] *Ibid., Spiegel Online.*
See also: *Sidney Morning Herald,* Dec. 29, 2007:
http://www.smh.com.au/news/environment/the-plastic-killing-fields/
2007/12/28/1198778702627.html?page=fullpage

[100] *Wasser und Mehr,* Oct. 29, 2006. Originally in *Süddeutsche Zeitung,* Oct. 28, 2006:
http://www.wasser-und-mehr.de/doc/aktuelles/088-meereszonen.html

[101] *Science Daily,* Aug. 14, 2006:
http://www.sciencedaily.com/releases/2006/08/060812155855.htm

[102] *Süddeutsche Zeitung,* Nov. 5, 2007:
http://www.sueddeutsche.de/wissen/artikel/621/141316/
See also: http://en.wikipedia.org/wiki/Three_Gorges_Dam

[103] *Amnesty – Magazin für Menschenrechte,* Feb. 2008:
http://www.amnesty.ch/de/aktuell/magazin/53/drei-schluchten-stau
damm-zwangsumsiedlung-china
See also: *International Rivers,* Oct. 13, 2007:
http://internationalrivers.org/en/china/three-gorges-dam/millions-
more-be-moved-three-gorges-dam

[104] Related information: *Time Magazine,* July 5, 1999:
http://www.purefood.org/Toxic/eufactfarm.cfm

[105] *University of Minnesota* (This is an extensive website on endocrine disruptors, click on the various headings):
http://enhs.umn.edu/5200/estrogen/index.html

[106] *Department for Environment, Food and Rural Affairs, Great Britain:*
http://www.defra.gov.uk/environment/chemicals/hormone/index.
htm#2

[107] *Telegraph.co.uk,* Oct. 6, 2008:
http://www.telegraph.co.uk/earth/earthnews/3352897/Red-List-of-
endangered-species—thousands-of-species-at-risk-of-disappear
ing.html

[108] Sebastian Siebert, *Terra-Alexander-Datenbank, Infoblatt Artensterben und Artenschutz,* Verlag Klett-Perthes, Gotha, 2003.

[109] For up-to-date Red List: http://www.iucnredlist.org/

[110] Excellent info under: http://rainforests.mongabay.com/

[111] *Spiegel Online,* Mar. 13, 2007:
http://www.spiegel.de/wissenschaft/natur/0,1518,471559,00.html
See also:
http://www.fao.org/newsroom/en/news/2007/1000506/index.html

[112] *WWF,* Mar. 2007:
http://assets.wwf.ch/downloads/studie_waelder_der_welt__ein_zustandsbericht_2007.pdf

[113] *Spiegel Online,* Feb. 6, 2008:
http://www.spiegel.de/wissenschaft/mensch/0,1518,533034,00.html

[114] *Pro-Regenwald:*
http://www.pro-regenwald.org/fb10ross.pdf

[115] *ORF:*
http://science.orf.at/science/news/123917

[116] *Spiegel Online,* Oct. 24, 2007:
http://www.spiegel.de/wissenschaft/natur/0,1518,513113,00.html
Proceedings of the Royal Society B, Jan. 7, 2008 275, 47–53:
http://rspb.royalsocietypublishing.org/content/275/1630/47.full.pdf+html?sid=9bd97bb6-2fb3-4201-8463-405b9f3e4ef4

[117] *Suddeutsche Zeitung,* Feb. 26, 2008:
http://www.sueddeutsche.de/wissen/artikel/600/160164/
See also:
Wikipedia: http://en.wikipedia.org/wiki/ Svalbard_Global_Seed_Vault

[118] *ARTE* (German public television station) July 5, 2008:
http://www.arte.tv/de/Willkommen/woche/244,broadcastingNum=
861459,day=1,week=28,year=2008.html

[119] *Times Online*, Mar. 9, 2008:
http://www.timesonline.co.uk/tol/news/uk/science/article3511818.ece

[120] *Cornell Chronicle Online*, Aug. 2, 2007:
http://www.news.cornell.edu/stories/Aug07/moreDiseases.sl.html
Spiegel Online, Aug. 14, 2007:
http://www.spiegel.de/wissenschaft/natur/0,1518,499781,00.html

[121] *Environmental News Network*, Dec. 10, 2007, from *Reuters*:
http://www.enn.com/climate/article/26898

[122] *taz.de,* Mar. 14, 2008:
http://www.taz.de/1/zukunft/umwelt/artikel/1/klimawandel-als-
sicherheits risiko/?src=AR&cHash=c362046563
The Guardian, Mar. 10, 2008:
http://www.guardian.co.uk/environment/2008/mar/10/climate
change.eu
Christian Science Monitor, Mar. 13&14, 2008:
http://www.csmonitor.com/2008/0313/p16s02-sten.html
http://www.csmonitor.com/2008/0314/p06s01-wogn.html?page=1

[123] *Deutschland Radio*, Apr. 2, 2008:
http://www.dradio.de/dkultur/sendungen/interview/762826/
See also: *Greenpeace,* June 19, 2007:
http://www.greenpeace.de/themen/klima/nachrichten/artikel/klima
fluechtlinge ignoriert und verleugnet/

[124] *International Alert,* Nov. 2007:
http://www.international-alert.org/publications/pub.php?p=322

[125] *Bavarian Ministry for Environment, Health and Consumer Affairs.*
Press release, Apr. 11, 2008:
http://www.comet.bayern.de/webservice/stmugv presse pdf/pdf
presse.php?tid=14166

[126] *University of Zurich, Geology Dept.* "Information über Felsstürze im Hochgebirge":
http://www.geo.uzh.ch/oldphys/research/faqs_felsstuerze.shtml

[127] *Spiegel Online,* July 14, 2006:
http://www.spiegel.de/wissenschaft/natur/0,1518,426694,00.html

[128] *Spiegel Online,* Nov. 11, 2004:
http://www.spiegel.de/wissenschaft/natur/0,1518,327309,00.html
The Independent, Apr. 17, 2002:
http://www.independent.co.uk/news/world/asia/melting-glaciers-in-himalayas-threaten-catastrophic-floods-657506.html

[129] *Spiegel Online,* Dec. 18, 2006:
http://www.spiegel.de/wissenschaft/natur/0,1518,455139,00.html

[130] *WDR*(German television station), Jan. 3, 2006:
http://www.wdr.de/tv/quarks/sendungsbeitraege/2006/0103/004_eis.jsp

[131] *ISDR,* Disaster statistics:
http://www.unisdr.org/disaster-statistics/pdf/isdr-disaster-statistics-occurrence.pdf

[132] *World Stress Map*:
http://www-wsm.physik.uni-karlsruhe.de/pub/stress_data/stress_data_frame.html
Bill McGuire, *The Independent,* Nov. 9, 2005:
http://www.independent.co.uk/environment/bill-mcguire-prophet-of-doom-514574.html
Welt.de, Jan. 1, 2006:
http://cires.colorado.edu/~bilham/ and www.innovations-report.de/html/berichte/geowissenschaften/bericht-18136.html
Roger Bilham, *University of Colorado News*:
http://cires.colorado.edu/news/press/2008/sichuanProvinceEarthquake.html

[133] *Desert USA,* Apr. 15, 2008:
http://www.desertusa.com/desertblog/?p=2305

[134] *Innovations Report,* Nov. 21, 2007:
http://www.innovations-report.de/html/berichte/geowissenschaften/bericht-96552.html
Report in English:
http://www.ruhr-uni-bochum.de/en-gruppe/PDFS/Hampel_etal_Geology_2007+suppl_mat.pdf

[135] *Munich Re Group*:
http://www.munichre.com/en/ts/geo_risks/natural_catastrophes_and_risks/volcanism/default.aspx

[136] *New Scientist,* April 3, 2008:
http://www.newscientist.com/article/dn13583

[137] *Zeit-wissen,* 02/06:
http://www.zeit.de/zeit-wissen/2005/05/Katastrophen.xml

[138] *Focus Online,* Feb. 9, 2007:
http://www.focus.de/wissen/wissenschaft/klima/frage-von-klaus-seibel_aid_28161.html

[139] *BR Bavarian Radio Online*, Jan. 4, 2007:
http://www.br-online.de/wissen/forschung/feuerspucker-DID119280148219180/vulkane-deutschland-eifel-ID671192801460156902.xml

[140] *British Geological Society*, "Hazardous Effects of Super-eruptions":
http://www.geolsoc.org.uk/gsl/education/page3042.html
See also:
http://en.wikipedia.org/wiki/Yellowstone_Caldera

[141] NASA: *Science@NASA,* "The Earth's Inconstant Magnetic Field," Dec. 29, 2003:
http://science.nasa.gov/headlines/y2003/29dec_magneticfield.htm?list9093

[142] *Cause and Development of All Illness*, Publishing House The Word, the Universal Spirit, Woodbridge, CT. 06525, USA, 2008. (German original published in 1986)

[143] FAO, Nov. 2007:
ftp://ftp.fao.org/docrep/fao/010/A0701E/A0701E00.pdf

[144] *Water for Food, Water for Life: A Comprehensive Assessment of Water Management in Agriculture.* London, 2007. Earthscan, and Colombo: International Water Management Institute:
http://www.fao.org/nr/water/docs/Summary_SynthesisBook.pdf

[145] *ORF,* Feb. 22, 2007:
http://science.orf.at/science/news/147349

[146] *Reuters,* Nov. 3, 2006:
http://www.iol.co.za/index.php?from=rss_SciTech%20Environment & set_id=1&click_id=143&art_id=qw1162501924478B251

[147] Kugler, Schneider, Groß, Wirr, Herff (Physicians at HG Naturklinik), *Vegetarisch essen – Fleisch vergessen...,* Verlag Das Wort, Marktheidenfeld, Germany, 2007. (not available in English)

[148] *Nature Magazine,* Feb. 21, 2008, v. 451, pp. 990-994.
Science Daily, Feb. 21, 2008:
http://www.sciencedaily.com/releases/2008/02/080220132611.htm

[149] *Baltimore Business Journal,* Feb. 5, 2004:
http://coloquio.com/coloquioonline/2004/0402dewitt.htm

[150] *ORF*: http://science.orf.at/science/news/114040
See also:
http://www.organicconsumers.org/madcow/times21604.cfm

[151] Wikipedia: http://en.wikipedia.org/wiki/Spanish_flu

[152] Wikipedia: http://www.avert.org/worldstats.htm

[153] Wikipedia: http://en.wikipedia.org/wiki/OPV_AIDS_hypothesis

[154] *AIDS WEEKLY Plus*, Sept. 28, 1998:
http://www.aegis.org/pubs/aidswkly/1998/AW980913.html

[155] *BBC News,* Mar. 19, 2004:
http://news.bbc.co.uk/2/hi/health/3520968.stm

[156] May be ordered free from:
Universal Life, The Inner Religion, P. O. Box 3549, Woodbridge, CT 06525, USA.

[157] G. Berz, *Naturkatastrophen im 21. Jahrhundert – Trends und Schadenpotentiale,* Münchener Rück, 2001, p. 259.

[158] *Ibid.,* p. 253.

Books in the Universal Life Series

This Is My Word –
A and Ω – The Gospel of Jesus
The Christ Revelation,
which true Christians the world over have come to know

A book that lets you really get to know about Jesus, the Christ, about the truth of His activity and life as Jesus of Nazareth. From the contents: The falsification of the teachings of Jesus of Nazareth during the past 2000 years - Jesus loved the animals and always spoke up for them - Meaning and purpose of a life on earth - Jesus taught about marriage - God is not a wrathful God - The teaching of "eternal damnation" is a mockery of God - Life after death - Equality between men and women - The coming times and the future of mankind, and much more!

1078 pages / Order No. S 007en / ISBN: 978-1-890841-17-1

The Message from the All
The Prophecy of God Today - Not the Word of the Bible
Volume 1

God does not forsake humankind, His children. He again speaks His direct word through Gabriele, whom He calls His prophetess and messenger, and gives answers to the basic questions of humankind, particularly to the spiritual correlations that are not explained in the Bible: on the meaning and purpose of life on earth, on the freedom of every being, on cause and effect, on the immortal soul and reincarnation, on Christ's deed of redemption, on the infinite love of God for every person and for all of creation, and much, much more.

Fourteen such revelations have been selected from the treasury of divine revelations and published for the first time.

The light of the eternal truth shines into our time, so that each one may recognize what God has to say to him, and, if he wants to, apply it in his life.

187 pages / Order No. S 137en / ISBN: 978-1-890841-36-2

The Word of the Christ of God –
to Mankind Before this World Passes Away
Nearer to God In You

Believe, trust, hope and endure! What do these mean and how can we apply them on our way to God? How do we turn belief into an active faith? How do we develop trust? Hope is expressed in setting goals that are carried out with confidence. What does it mean to endure in the divine sense? Experience the Inner Path in condensed form. Simple clear words, given to all people who long for God and a fulfilled, happy life in freedom. A gift from God to all His human children.

112 pages / Order No. S 139en / ISBN: 978-1-890841-45-4

The Path to Cosmic Consciousness –
Happiness, Freedom and Peace

The path to cosmic consciousness is the path to inner happiness and inner peace, to the feeling of having "arrived." Where? In the Kingdom of God, of which Jesus, the Christ, already taught, that it can be found within, in every person. It is our true, divine being. This is a path of liberation, which Gabriele, the prophetess and messenger of God, walked ahead of us. As a guide, she showed how we can learn not only to fulfill our work more quickly and conscientiously, but also how we can make peace with our fellowman and with nature and the animals, and how we can maintain it. Through this, we become happy and free!

75 pages / Order No. S 341en / ISBN: 978-1-890841-60-7

The Sermon on the Mount –
Life in Accordance With the Law of God

Timeless instructions for a peaceful and fulfilled life. A path that leads the way out of the dead-end in which so many people find themselves today. An excerpt from the work of revelation "This Is My Word."

112 pages / Order No. S 008en / ISBN: 978-1-890841-42-3

Live the Moment –
and You Will See and Recognize Yourself

Now, in this instant, the state of our soul shows itself. We can see it in our feelings, thoughts, words and actions that take place at every moment in us. Become sensitive to the signals of your inner life, because each day is a unique chance. And so, live the moment and become aware of what it wants to say to you.

76 pages / Order No. S 315en / ISBN: 978-1-890841-54-6

God Heals

There is a mighty, indescribable power in us. It is the central power of love, God's power and healing. Learn how this power in you can be unfolded!

From the content: God is eternally the same: Love, power, harmony and healing - God wants us to be healthy - Activating the inner forces - Effective prayer - Stillness and silence -What actually is illness? – It is based on wrong thinking -

61 pages / Order No. S 309en / ISBN: 978-1-890841-23-2

Cause and Development of All Illness
What a person sows, he will reap

A book more relevant than ever before, more exciting than a thriller, more moving than a documentary ... Many details revealed over 20 years ago by the Spirit of God are confirmed today by science: Without a healthy, balanced relationship between human beings, animals, plants and minerals, mankind will not survive in the long run. What does this mean for the future? What are the effects of man's destructive behavior toward nature, the animals and, not least, his own state of health? Learn about until now unknown correlations and frontier zones between spirit and matter, about the effect of the power of thoughts on our life, for instance, how harmful parasites and pathogens can be created by our behavior patterns, about holistic healing, the meaning of life on earth, and much more ...

360 pages / Order No. S 117en / ISBN: 978-1-890841-37-9

Life with our Animal Brothers and Sisters
You, the Animal – You, the Human Being

This is a book that describes the relationship between people and animals under a totally new perspective. Did you ever think that your pet senses exactly how you are feeling and reacts to this, and that it can even be influenced by your way of thinking and living? What is really the cause when an animal attacks a person? Is it really a wild animal that should be chained, or did the person who was "scented" by the animal also contribute to this? These are new aspects that help us to live more consciously and in true community with animals.

This book gives many suggestions and practical hints how we - based on a deep and selfless connection to our "animal brothers and sisters" - can live with them, so that they feel well with us. A book not only for animal friends, but also for people who want to develop a deep connection to nature.

108 pages / Order No. S 133en / ISBN: 978-1-890841-25-6

The Animal-Friendly Cookbook

Over the course of a lifetime, a person can save the lives of 450 animals, simply by not eating meat. This alone gives good reason to become vegetarian, or vegan! The bonus? You remain healthy and fit! This book is meant to serve all who want to contribute less and less to our world's environmental problems, to suffering in slaughterhouses and inhumane conditions in factory farming. There are no animal products in the recipes in this book!

208 pages / High-gloss ill. / Order No. S 436en / ISBN: 978-89041-57-7

Where Did I Come From? Where Am I Going?

The wherefrom and whereto of our life is no longer a mystery. Following explanations on the important questions on life after death, answers are given to 75 most frequently asked questions on this topic.

76 pages / Order No. S 407en / ISBN: 978-1-890841-09-6

Your Child and You -
The School of Life of Selfless Love
Every soul comes into this world with different capabilities, talents and qualities, but also with different soul burdens and base human tendencies and emotions. If these qualities, talents and capabilities of the soul as well as what it lacks are recognized in time, then the positive can be supported and the unlawful corrected in time. An invaluable book for raising children in the right way. With ground-breaking knowledge about spiritual correlations and many specific answers to practical questions.

108 pages / Order No. S 110en / ISBN: 978-89041-62-1

Ten Little Black Boys
A wonderful allegory of great spiritual depth. "Here is an insightful allegory of a journey to wholeness, a journey that should be made by everyone... It tells a story of discovery, of God and the mission we have to bring God's commandments to our fellow seekers by first applying them in our own lives. A very special experience for anyone seeking the Spirit of Life, the Creator."

74 pages / Color ill. / Order No. S 610en / ISBN: 978-1-890841-58-4

Who Is Sitting on the Chair of Peter
Only for the Clever and Analytical Mind - Vol. 1
A highly explosive reading! If, in view of the media spectacle put on by the Vatican, doubts should come up as to what all that has in the least to do with Jesus, the Christ, we become all the more incensed to learn how the teaching and structure of the Church directly stems from pagan idolatry. A "Christian" mantle has been draped over this cult of idolatry, thus, effectively duping humankind for centuries and still today. The Church interferes mightily, not only in the life of the individual but in all aspects of public life – by threatening the torments of hell for all those who do not subjugate themselves to it. This has nothing to do with Jesus, with His simple teaching and original Christianity.

232 pages / Order No. S 371en / ISBN: 978-1-890841-44-7

Books by Gabriele, the Prophetess of God

The Youth and the Prophet

Pirouettes of Life.
My fate, your fate, our fate. Whose life plan?

The Old-Timer and the Prophet

Servile Faith and Its Mysteries

Building the Divine Work of the Deed – Business
Management According to the Sermon on the Mount

Animals Lament - The Prophet Denounces!

The Murder of Animals Is the Death of Humans

God's Word, the Law of Love and Unity,
and Those of the Earth Without Rights

The Love for God and Neighbor
and a Bent, Distorted Christianity

To order: www.universal-spirit.org
1-800-846-2691
P.O. Box 3549, Woodbridge, CT 06525, USA
or: P.O. Box 5643, 97006 Wuerzburg, Germany

... put in
a nutshell...!

Gabriele Letter 1

December 2002: The Gabriele Letters are meant to make alert people aware of how weak in character and schizophrenic our society has become and that the majority of people simply thoughtlessly and numbly accept what the upper ranks of society tell them – Advent and Christmas have become a traditional pagan custom – "Hunter's Jargon": War against the animals – Why do the animals have to serve as a holiday repast? – All this has nothing to do with Jesus, the Christ – and much more.

Gabriele Letter 2

January 2003: Highlights on the development of church history – The pope's statement "God has withdrawn into heaven, disgusted with humanity's actions" is a declaration of bankruptcy by the Church – God is not silent. He has spoken at all times through enlightened men and women – The true God never dwelt in churches of stone – God never blessed weapons – God never let Himself be "represented" by a human being – The true God cannot be bribed. He is absolute. His being is love and love dwells in each human being, in all forms of life in the nature kingdoms – and much more.

Gabriele Letter 3

March 2003: The love for God and neighbor and bent, distorted Christendom – The human being, the image of God – Equality, freedom, unity, brotherliness and justice: The basis for a peaceable life with one another – A person's talents – Are the church institutions against war? Violence, to create peace? – Most people are conformists. The creation of dependency is a fundamental component of the "church system" – The "consortium Church," an unholy alliance with the State – Every state authority "instituted by God"? – No salvation outside the Church? – The commandments of God in a reflection on church doctrine – Divine justice and human law – Reincarnation: an early Christian knowledge – and much more.

The Large Gabriele Letter 4

July 2003: The Word of God, the Law of Love and Unity, and Those of This Earth Without Rights: The harmonious order of the Eternal in His creation, when mankind does not interfere – The "black majesty" speaks: Make the earth subject to you, violently! – Christian churches have brought only suffering, hardship and death to man, nature and animals – From the intellect to understanding and comprehension – Th animal, a wonderful creature from God's hand – Experiencing the unity of life in nature – Expeditions into nature – Encounters with the "dangerous wild pigs" – Deer, fox and hedgehog mothers proudly show off their children – and much more.